BREADS & BAKES

First published in Great Britain by Simon & Schuster UK Ltd, 2003
A Viacom Company

Simon & Schuster UK Ltd
Africa House
64–78 Kingsway
London
WC2B 6AH

1 3 5 7 9 10 8 6 4 2

Design: **Fiona Andreanelli**
Typesetting: **Stylize Digital Artwork**
Food photography: **Steve Baxter**
Home economist: **Joy Skipper**
Stylist for food photography: **Liz Belton**
Editor: **Paula Borton**
Printed and bound in China

ISBN 0 74324 011 1

Best-kept Secrets of the Women's Institute

BREADS & BAKES

Carrie O'Regan & Jill Brand

SIMON & SCHUSTER
A VIACOM COMPANY

CONTENTS

INTRODUCTION

Bread is a staple food in many countries around the world and comes in a wonderful variety of types and shapes.

Bread was first produced once our ancestors started to understand the growing of wheat, thought to have begun before 7000 BC in the regions of Anatolia, Iran and Syria. The grain needed to be ground and so milling techniques developed over several centuries, from the most primitive technique of just using flat stones to crush the grains to mills driven by water-power. The first breads were flat, unleavened ones but, once the action of yeast was discovered, probably in Ancient Egypt, though this is not known for certain, most breads were leavened.

One of the joys of baking is coming into a house with that wonderful aroma of fresh bread. It has even been claimed by estate agents that this aroma will help sell your house. Although bread-making often seems labour-intensive and time-consuming, it is actually easy to do and can be fitted in round other tasks at home. The pleasure of eating your own home-made bread and the savings you make will be well worth the effort.

Bread-making can also be very relaxing. If you have never attempted baking bread, firstly set aside some time so that your first session is not hurried and stressful. Walk along any supermarket aisle or look in the baker's shop window and you will see a vast range of breads from around the world. These newly trendy breads are much cheaper made at home, and this also opens up the possibility of experimenting with interesting and unusual ingredients

When making bread, a handy tip is to keep a couple of clean plastic bags fluffed up and open, so if the phone rings or there's a knock at the door you can just slip your hands into the bags and avoid getting flour all over the phone or the door handle.

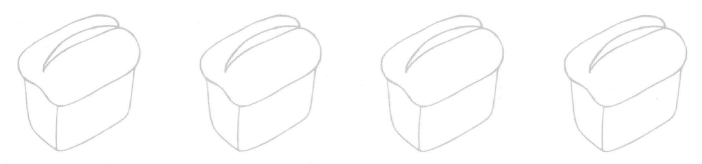

STEP-BY-STEP BREAD-MAKING

PREPARING THE YEAST

Yeast is a single-celled organism and needs four conditions if it is to begin dividing and growing, which is how it raises the dough. Sugar gives an initial supply of food, which starts fermentation. The hand-hot liquid added in the recipe gives moisture and a suitable temperature for the yeast to start working. Too much heat will destroy the yeast though, so it is important that the liquid is not too hot. Lastly, time is needed for the fermentation process to be completed.

USING DIFFERENT TYPES OF YEAST

- Using fresh yeast: Cream the yeast with a little sugar. Add the hand-hot liquid and leave to stand until frothy.
- Using dried yeast: Sprinkle the yeast and sugar on to the hand-hot liquid and leave to stand until frothy.
- Using easy-blend yeast: There is no need to prepare this before use. It is sprinkled into the mix of flour, salt and fat at the start of the process.

MIXING THE DOUGH

Sift the flour, salt and any spices into a bowl to add air and remove lumps. If you are using a wholemeal or country-grain flour, stir the bran and grains left in the sieve into the flour after sieving. Rub in any fat and stir all the other dry ingredients into the flour, followed by enough of the liquid to form a soft dough. The proteins in the flour absorb the liquid and develop an elastic substance called gluten, which forms the structure of the crumb in the finished bread as it stretches.

KNEADING

Turn the dough on to a lightly floured surface and knead it by drawing the sides into the centre, giving the dough a quarter-turn and pushing it away with the heel of your hand and then drawing the sides in again, until the dough is smooth and elastic. This will take about 10 minutes. At this stage the dough will have a more even texture and the gluten will be developed, allowing the dough to rise evenly.

If you have a food mixer or food processor with a dough hook, this can be used to mix and knead the dough according to the manufacturer's instruction book. Kneading dough by hand is very satisfying but also tiring, and if you're doing several things at once a machine with a dough hook can be a real boon.

RISING

Put the dough in a greased bowl or bag, cover with a greased polythene bag, oiled clingfilm or a damp tea-towel (this prevents a hard crust from forming) and leave in a warm place to rise until doubled in size. The ambient temperature will affect the length of time the dough needs to rise, for example, if you leave it in an airing cupboard, by a boiler or in the top oven it will rise more quickly than if left on a work surface. It is important the bowl does not have direct contact with a source of heat, as this will destroy the yeast. During the rising stage the yeast multiplies and carbon dioxide bubbles form, pushing the dough up. The gluten stretches, becoming soft and more elastic; when the dough is properly risen it will not spring back if a finger is inserted in it. If the dough is allowed to rise too much though, it will collapse. To prevent this, check it regularly and do not let it more than double in size. Depending on the ambient temperature this takes 1½–2 hours.

It is also possible to leave dough to rise in the fridge overnight. The low temperatures give a very slow, long rising that produces an excellent finished taste and texture.

SECOND KNEADING OR 'KNOCKING BACK'

Any large bubbles of carbon dioxide are broken down into smaller ones of a more even size when the dough is knocked back. Turn the dough on to a floured surface and knead by drawing the edges into the centre just as for the initial kneading.

If you have used easy-blend yeast, speed up the process by omitting the first rising and knocking back, moving straight from kneading to shaping the dough.

SECOND RISING OR 'PROVING'

Cut and/or shape the dough as required, without over stretching it as this can cause the dough to become misshapen when baked. Place in the appropriate greased tin or on a greased baking sheet and cover as before. Leave the dough in a warm place again to prove, until it has doubled in size. During this time the yeast fermentation process continues and more carbon dioxide is formed.

BAKING

Bread dough should be put into a preheated hot oven and will continue to rise at the beginning of the cooking time. The yeast is then killed by the heat and the dough bakes in the shape that it had formed when the yeast was killed.

To test whether bread is ready, tap the sides and base – if the sound is hollow the bread is cooked. Remove the bread from the tin and transfer to a wire rack to cool.

BREAD-MAKING PROBLEMS AND REMEDIES

HEAVY, DENSE BREAD

- Yeast too old – check date on yeast.
- Liquid used too hot and yeast was destroyed – use hand-hot liquid.
- Dough left to rise or prove in direct contact with a source of heat – place a wire rack under bowl to avoid direct contact.
- Not enough liquid used, so dough is too dry – check recipe quantities.
- Insufficient time given for rising and proving – allow to rise for longer.

UNEVEN TEXTURE

- Not kneaded enough after first rising, so gas bubbles not broken down evenly – knead until dough has a smooth appearance.
- Oven too cool when bread first put in – check oven temperature on recipe; or buy or borrow an oven thermometer and check the actual temperature of your oven. Bear in mind that fan ovens usually cook at a higher temperature than ordinary electric or gas ovens, so make sure you are using the correct temperature.

WRINKLED SURFACE

- Dough left to prove for too long, so gluten over stretched and collapsed – reduce proving time.
- Oven too cool when bread first put in – check what temperature is specified in the recipe and check your oven's temperature as above.

SOUR TASTE

- Yeast old and stale – check date on yeast.
- Too much yeast used in proportion to flour – check recipe quantities.
- Dough over risen or over proved – reduce time for rising and proving.

INGREDIENTS

BREAD-MAKING INGREDIENTS

ASCORBIC ACID
Ascorbic acid or Vitamin C is bought in tablets and helps the fermentation of yeast. It is often added to easy-blend yeast to help it to work.

CHOCOLATE
Chocolate for baking can be found on the home-baking shelves of most supermarkets, or you can choose from the confectionery shelves. There is usually a selection of milk, white and plain (bitter) chocolate and chocolate chips. Plain (bitter) chocolate must contain a minimum of 30% cocoa solids; obviously the more cocoa solids, the stronger the flavour. Continental dark chocolate can contain over 70% cocoa solids.

CITRUS FRUIT
When the zest of citrus fruit – lemons, limes and oranges – is to be used, try to buy fruit with unwaxed skins.

COCOA POWDER
Cocoa has quite a bitter flavour and can be used in baking to flavour a whole dough with chocolate (as opposed to adding pieces of chocolate).

DRIED FRUIT, BASIC (currants, raisins, sultanas and glacé cherries)
These can now be bought ready cleaned, but it is probably still worthwhile sorting through the fruit to remove any stalks, etc. Glacé cherries should be washed and dried.

DRIED FRUIT, EXOTIC (apricots, mango, papaya and pineapple)
These new fruits, which have become available because of increased production and improved drying methods in their countries of origin, add considerable excitement to breads and other baking. They are generally ready to eat and do not need soaking. If you buy the ordinary 'dried' fruit instead of the 'ready-to-eat' version, however, you will need to soak it in a little water for an hour to make it fleshy, before adding to the mixture.

EGGS
These should be used at room temperature and, for all recipes in this book, medium eggs have been used unless stated otherwise in the individual recipes.

FATS AND OILS (butter, lard, margarine and spreads)
Fats remain solid at room temperature. Oils are the refined end product of a nut- or seed-crushing process, and are used for cooking when a recipe needs something that remains liquid at room temperature. Oils and fats can both be used in bread-making and they give different flavours to doughs. Oils are often used in continental breads, such as the Italian ones that are so popular now, for example ciabatta and foccacia; olive oil gives the best flavour.

Butter is available salted, slightly salted or unsalted; all these recipes use slightly salted butter unless otherwise stated. Unsalted butter gives the very best flavour and should be used in delicate, sweet breads such as croissants and brioches.

Margarine which, if full fat, has to contain not less than 80% fat. This will act in the same way as butter when spread or cooked with. **Hard margarines** are made with a blend of hydrogenated fish oils and vegetable oils. The blend is perfect for baking, particularly for traditional methods. This type of margarine is best used when it needs to be rubbed in. **Soft margarines** are also made with a blend of hydrogenated fish oils and vegetable oils, but are especially blended (emulsified) to give a softer consistency. It is most important that they are used straight from the refrigerator. If soft margarines are allowed to soften before use, the cooked result will be poor.

Spreads have a lower fat content than margarines – somewhere between 60% and 80%. They are made from a mixture of ingredients: animal fats, hydrogenated fish oils, vegetable oils and dairy ingredients, according to the individual brand. Packet spreads are best used straight from the refrigerator and perform well in traditional recipes. Like hard margarines, they are an alternative to butter.

Alternatives to animal products for those who wish to avoid animal fats or other ingredients of animal origin, either for religious, dietary or cultural reasons, are available made from vegetable, nut and herb oils. Similarly, for those unable to tolerate milk products, there are milk-free varieties available.

FLOUR

It is always a good idea to sift flour before using it; this will ensure that any impurities are sieved out, and that it mixes better with the other ingredients, such as salt, raising agents or ground spices.

White self-raising flour has raising agents thoroughly mixed into the flour so that a consistent result is obtained.

White plain flour is suitable for most scones and bakes when used with a raising agent.

Wholemeal flour can be substituted for white flour. For a lighter result, use half wholemeal and half white flour.

Strong bread flour is made from blends of hard wheat containing higher percentages of gluten. This becomes elastic and stretches, giving a good structure to the finished loaf. Strong flour can be bought as white (all the bran and wheatgerm is removed), brown (the outer layers of the bran are removed) and wholemeal (contains all the wheat grain). Country-grain flours have whole grains or flakes added.

Rye flour is made from a cereal that grows particularly well in colder climates and is used more in bread-making in northern Europe and Russia. Breads made from rye flour are darker in colour and have a denser texture.

Gluten-free flour is usually a mixture of rice, potato, buckwheat and maize flours and is suitable for those with a gluten intolerance.

Polenta is an Italian golden cornmeal produced from maize.

MILK

The recipes in this book use cow's milk, unless stated in the recipe and either whole or semi-skimmed can be used. For bread recipes it is best if milk is at a hand-hot temperature.

NUTS (almonds, brazils, hazels, walnuts)

These are all available, shelled, in packets from supermarkets. Almonds, already skinned, are available whole, flaked or ground. Brazils and hazels are available whole. Walnuts are available as halves or in pieces and the latter are especially useful when they are to be chopped.

RAISING AGENTS

Bicarbonate of soda is an alkaline substance that gives off carbon dioxide to assist with the rising of food.

Cream of tartar is an acidic substance which is usually mixed two parts to one part bicarbonate of soda, and reacts to release the carbon dioxide slowly giving a more even rise. It leaves behind a tasteless salt in the food.

Baking powder is a mixture of the two, blended with dried starch to stop a reaction of the two mixtures while the baking powder is stored.

YEAST

Yeast is a minute single-celled plant visible only under the microscope. It feeds on carbohydrates (starches and sugars) present in flour. Given the right conditions of food, moisture and warmth, yeast produces carbon dioxide gas to raise the dough, making it spongy and light, and alcohols to flavour it. Yeast for home-baking can be bought in three forms, compressed fresh yeast, dried active baking yeast or easy-blend dried yeast. 25 g (1 oz) fresh yeast = 15 g (½ oz) or 15 ml (1 tablespoon) dried yeast or 2 sachets of easy-blend dried yeast.

Fresh yeast is quick and easy to use, but can be difficult to obtain. It is usually available from health food shops, some master bakers and supermarkets. Fresh yeast should be cool and firm to the touch. It will keep for up to two weeks in a refrigerator if stored in a small plastic container or loosely wrapped in a polythene bag. Fresh yeast can also be frozen for up to six weeks (cold or freezing temperatures do not kill yeast – unlike hot ones – but they make it dormant). Freeze the yeast in small quantities so you can defrost only as much as you need at the time. Wrap each piece well and freeze quickly. Frozen yeast can be blended straight into the hand-hot liquid or allowed to thaw for 20 minutes before using.

Dried yeast is available in 100 g tubs from most supermarkets. Dried yeast will keep for up to a year in its unopened container. Once opened, though, it should be stored in a small airtight container and will generally remain active for about 4 months after opening. The larger the air space in the container, however, the less well the yeast will keep, so use the smallest airtight container available.

Easy-blend dried yeast comes in 7 g sachets and is added directly to the dry mix of flour, salt and fat (no reconstitution is required) and often contains ascorbic acid (vitamin C) to aid fermentation. This yeast can be substituted for fresh or dried yeast as long as you follow the manufacturer's instructions with regard to quantities and uses.

SALT
Added to bread recipes to give flavour, salt also prevents the yeast from working too quickly, thus forming a coarse crust. Too much salt, however, will inhibit the yeast action.

SUGAR
Commercially prepared sugars are all available in refined white or unrefined golden versions. Sugar in bread-making is mainly for activating the yeast and the type of sugar is not really so important as the quantities are small. In scones, muffins and tray bakes, however, the choice of sugar can affect the flavour of the finished article.

Caster sugar is a fine-grain sugar and is mostly used for baking.

Granulated sugar does not dissolve as easily as caster sugar, and in baking is mostly used for sprinkling over cakes as a crunchy topping.

Icing sugar is a finely ground powder and apart from icings is used sprinkled on top of dishes that are to be glazed under the grill.

Soft light and dark brown sugar refers to any fine moist brown sugar made from refined sugar combined with molasses. It is commonly used in baking and gives a slightly more toasty flavour than white sugar.

Muscovado (or Barbados) sugar is unrefined 'raw' cane sugar, available in light or dark versions. It is usually finely grained and gives bakes such as flapjacks a deeper flavour.

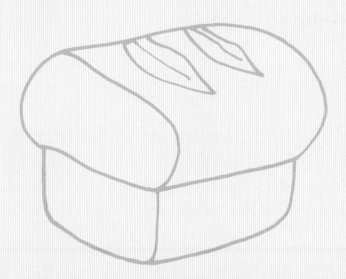

EQUIPMENT

TINS FOR BAKING BREAD

To avoid disasters, it is important that you use the correct tin for the recipe you wish to cook, and when selecting bread tins, the depth (the height of the sides of the tin) and diameter (the distance across the top of the tin) are both important.

The tins used in this book are:

Square with a usual depth of 4 cm (1¾ inches)
Loaf a rectangular tin, sold in 450 g (1 lb) or 900 g (2 lb) sizes
Swiss roll a rectangular tin, with a usual depth of 2 cm (¾ inches)
Patty/bun tins a shallow tin with 12 round indentations for making individual buns, etc
Muffin tins divided into 12 with a usual depth of 3 cm (1¼ inches)
Baking trays a flat tray, typically 30 cm by 22 cm (12 inches by 9 inches).

LINING TINS

When cooking breads it is not necessary to line the tin, though commercially produced liners are available for loaf tins if desired. When baking muffins, put the batter into individual paper cases in the shaped tins. For some of the tray bakes it is advisable to line the base of the tin.

FREEZING BREAD

Bread can be successfully frozen. It should be allowed to cool and then sealed in a polythene bag. It may be more convenient to slice loaves before freezing so individual slices can be taken out for use.

OVEN TEMPERATURES AND TIMINGS

Conventional electric ovens and gas ovens need to be preheated for 15 minutes before baked goods are put in them. Fan ovens do not need preheating unless a recipe specifically tells you to do this. In bread-making it is important to put the bread into a hot oven, so the yeast is destroyed quickly, so preheating is advised for all oven types. Cooking times are still quicker in a fan oven than a conventional oven. Although few cookery books give a different setting for fan ovens, expecting cooks to consult their cooker handbooks, temperatures are given for fan ovens in all recipes in this book.

Inevitably, each oven varies in its efficiency so, to obtain the best results from your oven, it may be necessary to adjust the instructions for cooking temperatures given in the recipes in this book: gas settings may have to be varied by one gas mark and electric or fan ovens by 10°–20°C.

When following the cooking times given in the recipes, use the approximate middle time if you are cooking in a gas or electric oven: i.e. if the time given is 10–20 minutes, check the cake at 15 minutes. When cooking in a fan oven, always check the cake at the earliest time: if the time given is 10–20 minutes, check at 10 minutes.

OVEN TEMPERATURES

Gas Mark (preheat for 15 minutes)	Electric (°C) (preheat for 15 minutes)	Fan oven (°C) (preheat only when indicated)
	80	60
	90	70
	100	80
E	110	90
1	120–140	100–120
2	150	130
3	160–170	140–150
4	180	160
5	190	170
6	200–210	180–190
7	220	200
8	230	210
9	240–250	220–230

NOTE: these temperatures are equivalent settings rather than exact conversions of degrees of heat.

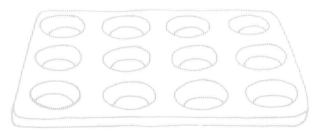
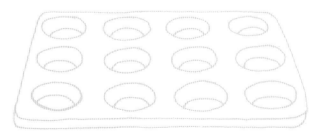

There's nothing like baking bread — the silky, supple feel of the dough as you knead it, the magical qualities of yeast and the wonderful aroma of baking loaves wafting through the kitchen. This chapter contains basic bread recipes, using a range of different flours and other ingredients to make breads for everyday use. The recipes show you how to use the three

BASIC DOUGH RECIPES

commonly available types of yeast: fresh, dried and easy-blend. There are also ideas for shaping that include tin loaves, plaits and rolls. Once you have mastered the basics, you can then go on to do some experimentation of your own.

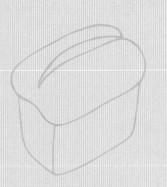
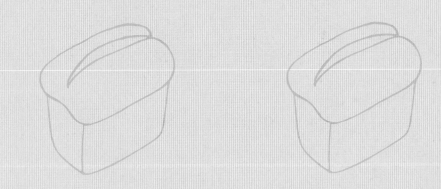

MAKES: a 900 g (2 lb) loaf
PREPARATION TIME: 25 minutes
+ activating yeast + rising
COOKING TIME: 30–40 minutes
FREEZING: recommended

Some brown breads can be very heavy. In this recipe, a mixture of flours is included to give a lighter texture to this brown loaf.

BASIC BROWN BREAD

15 g (½ oz) dried yeast
1 teaspoon sugar
450 ml (16 fl oz) hand-hot water
450 g (1 lb) strong brown flour
225 g (8 oz) strong white flour
2 teaspoons salt
25 g (1 oz) butter
beaten egg, to glaze (optional)

1 Mix the yeast and sugar with 150 ml (¼ pint) of the water in a small bowl. Leave until frothy, about 15–20 minutes.
2 In a bowl, sift the flours and salt. Cut the butter into small pieces and rub it into the flour until it resembles fine breadcrumbs.
3 Mix in the yeast mixture and then gradually stir in the rest of the water, mixing to form a rough ball.
4 Using your hands, draw the mixture together into a ball. Turn it out on to a floured surface.
5 Knead the dough for 8–10 minutes, until the dough is smooth, elastic and no longer sticky.

6 Oil or grease a 900 g (2 lb) loaf tin.
7 Press the dough out and shape to fit the tin.
8 Cover the tin with an oiled polythene bag and leave to rise in a warm place for about 1 hour, until doubled in size.
9 Preheat the oven to Gas Mark 7/electric oven 220°C/fan oven 200°C.
10 Before baking, dust the top of the loaf with flour for a soft crust or brush with beaten egg for a shiny crust
11 Bake for 30–40 minutes, until the loaf is golden and the base sounds hollow when tapped. Cool on a wire rack.

MAKES: a 900 g (2 lb) loaf
PREPARATION TIME: 25 minutes + rising
COOKING TIME: 30–40 minutes
FREEZING: recommended

This traditional recipe makes a **soft white loaf**. It's very simple and once you have mastered this try making several loaves at once and putting some in the freezer.

675 g (1½ lb) strong white flour
2 teaspoons salt
25 g (1 oz) butter
1 sachet easy-blend dried yeast
450 ml (16 fl oz) hand-hot water
beaten egg, to glaze (optional)

1. In a bowl, sift the flour and salt. Cut the butter into small pieces and rub it into the flour until it resembles fine breadcrumbs.
2. Mix in the yeast and gradually stir in the liquid, mixing to form a rough ball.
3. Using your hands, draw the mixture together into a ball. Turn it out on to a floured surface.
4. Knead the dough for 8–10 minutes until the dough is smooth, elastic and no longer sticky.
5. Oil or grease a 900 g (2 lb) loaf tin.
6. Press the dough out and shape to fit the tin.
7. Cover the tin with an oiled polythene bag and leave to rise in a warm place for about 1 hour, until doubled in size.
8. Before baking, dust the top of the loaf with flour for a soft crust or brush with beaten egg for a shiny crust. Preheat the oven to Gas Mark 7/electric oven 220°C/fan oven 200°C.
9. Bake for 30–40 minutes, until the loaf is golden and the base sounds hollow when tapped. Transfer to a wire rack to cool.

BASIC WHITE BREAD

MAKES a 900 g (2 lb) loaf
PREPARATION TIME: 25 minutes + rising
COOKING TIME: 30–40 minutes
FREEZING: recommended

WHOLEMEAL LOAF

Using 100% wholemeal flour gives this bread a rougher, **nutty texture**. This loaf makes wonderful toast.

675 g (1½ lb) strong wholemeal flour
1 tablespoon sugar
2 teaspoons salt
25 g (1 oz) butter
1 sachet easy-blend dried yeast
450 ml (16 fl oz) hand-hot water
beaten egg, to glaze (optional)

1 In a bowl, sift the flour, sugar and salt. Cut the butter into small pieces and rub into the flour until it resembles fine breadcrumbs.
2 Mix in the yeast, and gradually stir in the liquid, mixing to form a rough ball.
3 Using your hands, draw the mixture together into a ball. Turn on to a floured surface.
4 Knead the dough for 8–10 minutes, until the dough is smooth, elastic and no longer sticky.
5 Oil or grease a 900 g (2 lb) loaf tin.
6 Press the dough out and shape to fit the tin.
7 Cover the tin with an oiled polythene bag and leave to rise in a warm place for about 1 hour, until doubled in size.
8 Preheat the oven to Gas Mark 7/electric oven 220°C/fan oven 200°C.
9 Before baking, dust the top of the loaf with flour for a soft crust or brush with beaten egg for a shiny crust.
10 Bake for 30–40 minutes, until the loaf is golden and the base sounds hollow when tapped. Transfer to a wire rack to cool.

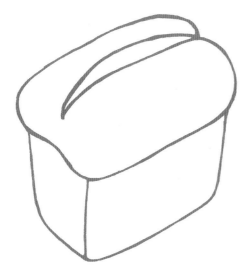

MAKES two 450 g (1 lb) coburgs
PREPARATION TIME: 25 minutes + rising
COOKING TIME: 30–40 minutes
FREEZING: recommended

GRANARY COB

This recipe uses a flour containing whole grains that gives a crunchy and nutty taste to the loaf, which is baked in a round shape traditionally called a cob or coburg.

675 g (1½ lb) country-grain flour
2 teaspoons salt
1 tablespoon sugar
25 g (1 oz) butter
1 sachet easy-blend dried yeast
450 ml (16 fl oz) hand-hot water
beaten egg, to glaze (optional)

1 In a bowl, sift the flour, salt and sugar. Cut the butter into small pieces and rub it into the flour until it resembles fine breadcrumbs.
2 Mix in the yeast and gradually stir in the liquid, mixing to form a rough ball.
3 Using your hands, draw the mixture together into a ball. Turn on to a floured surface.
4 Knead the dough for 8–10 minutes, until the dough is smooth, elastic and no longer sticky.
5 Oil or grease a baking tray.
6 Divide the dough into two, shape each into a smooth ball, flatten slightly. Cut a deep cross into the top of each coburg. Place on the greased baking tray. Cover the tin with an oiled polythene bag and leave to rise in a warm place for about 1 hour, until doubled in size.
7 Preheat the oven to Gas Mark 7/electric oven 220°C/fan oven 200°C.
8 Before baking, dust the top of the loaf with flour for a soft crust or brush with beaten egg for a shiny crust.
9 Bake for 30–40 minutes, until the loaf is golden and the base sounds hollow when tapped. Transfer to a wire rack to cool.

MAKES 6 rolls
PREPARATION TIME:
20–25 minutes + rising
COOKING TIME: 10–15 minutes
FREEZING: recommended

250 g (9 oz) mixture of strong brown
flour and strong white flour or 250 g
(9 oz) mixture of strong white flour and
country-grain flour or 250 g (9 oz)
mixture of strong wholemeal flour and
country-grain flour
1 teaspoon salt
25 g (1 oz) butter
1 teaspoon sugar
1 teaspoon easy-blend dried yeast
175 ml (6 fl oz) hand-hot milk

Flours can be mixed to give different textures to these rolls. Combining strong brown and strong white flour will give a soft bread texture; strong white and country-grain will give a soft texture with a nutty flavour and strong wholemeal and country-grain will give a coarser texture and a stronger nutty flavour.

1 Sift the flour and salt into a bowl. Rub in the butter.
2 Stir in the sugar and yeast. Add enough milk to form a soft dough. You may need more milk if using wholemeal flour.
3 Turn the dough on to a floured surface and knead well until the dough is smooth and elastic.
4 Place the dough in a clean, greased bowl, cover and leave to rise until doubled in size.
5 Preheat the oven to Gas Mark 7/electric oven 220°C/fan oven 200°C.
6 Knock back and divide the dough into six. Form into rolls (see below). Place on a greased baking tray and leave to prove for 30 minutes.
7 Bake for 10–15 minutes. Transfer to a wire rack to cool.

SHAPING ROLLS
Twist Form the dough into a sausage 30 cm (12 inches) long, fold in half and twist around itself.
Plait Divide the dough into three pieces. Form each into a sausage 12 cm (5 inches) long and plait together.
Knot Form the dough into a sausage 24 cm (9½ inches) long and tie it into a knot.
Cottage rolls Take a small piece from the dough and roll it into a ball. Form the larger piece into a round and place the smaller ball on top. Push a floured wooden spoon handle through the top to form an indentation.
'S' shape Form the dough into a sausage 18 cm (7 inches) long and bend into an 'S' shape, so the inside edges touch each other.
Coburg Form the dough into a flattened ball and cut a cross in the top, using a sharp knife.
Hedgehog Form the dough into an oval, making one end more pointed to form the nose. Using a pair of scissors, snip the dough to give the appearance of spines. Currants can be used for eyes, if you like.
Bap Form the dough into a ball, place on a baking tray and flatten with the palm of your hand. Dust with flour before baking.

MIXED-FLOUR ROLLS

MAKES an 18 cm (7-inch) ring
PREPARATION TIME: 25–30 minutes + rising
COOKING TIME: 20–30 minutes
FREEZING: recommended

RYE RING

Rye tends to produce a heavier bread, but mixing it with another flour gives this ring a lighter texture.

25 g (1 oz) margarine
200 ml (7 fl oz) hand-hot water
150 g (5 oz) rye flour
175 g (6 oz) strong wholemeal flour
1 teaspoon salt
½ sachet easy-blend yeast
1 tablespoon chopped fresh herbs
1 teaspoon poppy seeds

1 Melt the margarine in the water.
2 In a large bowl, sift the flours and salt together and then mix in the yeast and herbs.
3 Carefully pour in the liquid and mix to form a soft dough.
4 Turn out on to a floured surface and knead well for 10 minutes until smooth and elastic.
5 Place in a clean greased bowl, cover and leave in a warm place to double in size.
6 Knock back and knead again. Shape into a long sausage shape. Place on a greased baking tray, joining the ends to form a ring. Cover and leave to prove in a warm place, until doubled in size.
7 Preheat the oven to Gas Mark 6/electric oven 200°C/fan oven 180°C.
8 Make slits around the ring, brush the top with water and sprinkle with poppy seeds. Bake for 20–30 minutes, until well risen and golden in colour.
9 Transfer to a wire rack to cool.

MAKES 4 individual pizzas
PREPARATION TIME: 20–30 minutes + activating yeast + rising
COOKING TIME: 10–15 minutes
FREEZING: recommended

PIZZAS

This recipe was inspired by a visit to Rome where the pizzas have thin bases and mixed toppings. Thinly sliced Italian meats, olives and mushrooms top these individual pizzas.

15 g (½ oz) fresh yeast
1 teaspoon caster sugar
225 ml (8 fl oz) hand-hot milk
450 g (1 lb) strong white flour
½ teaspoon salt
50 g (2 oz) margarine
1 egg

FOR THE TOPPINGS:
250 g (9 oz) passata with garlic and herbs
4 slices of prosciutto crudo
4 slices of salami milano
8 stoned black olives
4 mushrooms, sliced
115 g (4 oz) mozzarella cheese

1. Cream the yeast and sugar in a small bowl. Add half the milk and leave until frothy, about 15–20 minutes.
2. Sift the flour and salt into a bowl. Rub in the margarine.
3. Add the egg, yeast mixture and enough of the remaining milk to form a soft dough.
4. Turn the dough on to a floured surface and knead well until the dough is smooth and elastic.
5. Place the dough in a clean, greased bowl, cover and leave to rise until doubled in size.
6. Preheat the oven to Gas Mark 7/electric oven 220°C/ fan oven 200°C.
7. Knock back and divide the dough into four. Roll each into a 20 cm (8-inch) round. Place on a greased baking tray.
8. Spread each base with passata and arrange the other ingredients on top, finishing with the cheese.
9. Bake for 10–15 minutes.

NOTE: Other toppings could include artichoke hearts, anchovies, prawns, tuna, salami, pepperoni, cooked chicken, peppers, pineapple, sweetcorn, black olives or capers. Choosing three to five toppings, plus cheese, works well.

MAKES a 450 g (1 lb) loaf
PREPARATION TIME:
35–40 minutes + activating yeast + rising
COOKING TIME: 30–40 minutes
FREEZING: recommended

Enriched dough contains milk and egg, giving it a closer texture and softer crust. This is good for making speciality breads.

ENRICHED SAVOURY BREAD

FOR THE YEAST BATTER:
2 teaspoons dried yeast or 15 g (½ oz)
fresh yeast
½ teaspoon caster sugar
5 tablespoons hand-hot milk
50 g (2 oz) strong white flour

FOR THE LOAF:
175 g (6 oz) strong white flour
½ teaspoon salt
25 g (1 oz) unsalted butter
1 egg, beaten
beaten egg, to glaze (optional)

1   To make the yeast batter using dried yeast, place the yeast and sugar in a small jug. Stir in the milk and leave for 5 minutes.

2   Stir in the flour and leave in a warm place until frothy (about 15–20 minutes).

3   Alternatively, to make the yeast batter using fresh yeast, place the yeast, sugar and milk in a small jug. Stir in the flour and leave in a warm place until frothy (about 15–20 minutes).

4   In a large bowl, sift together the flour and salt. Rub in the butter. Stir in the egg and the yeast batter and mix to give a soft dough.

5   Turn on to a floured surface and knead for 8–10 minutes, until the dough is smooth, elastic and no longer sticky.

6   Oil or grease a 450 g (1 lb) loaf tin. Press the dough out and shape to fit the tin. Cover the tin with an oiled polythene bag and leave to rise in a warm place for about 1 hour, until doubled in size.

7   Preheat the oven to Gas Mark 7/electric oven 220°C/fan oven 200°C.

8   Before baking, dust the top of the loaf with flour for a soft crust or brush with beaten egg for a shiny crust.

9   Bake for 30–40 minutes, until the loaf is golden and the base sounds hollow when tapped. Transfer to a wire rack to cool.

MAKES a 450 g (I lb) loaf
PREPARATION TIME:
35–40 minutes + activating yeast + rising
COOKING TIME: 30–40 minutes

This dough contains milk, egg and sugar, giving it a sweet taste and close texture. Breads such as brioches are made from this.

ENRICHED SWEET BREAD

FOR THE YEAST BATTER:
2 teaspoons dried yeast or 15 g (½ oz)
fresh yeast
½ teaspoon caster sugar
5 tablespoons hand-hot milk
50 g (2 oz) strong white flour

FOR THE LOAF:
175 g (6 oz) strong white flour
½ teaspoon salt
25 g (1 oz) caster sugar
25 g (1 oz) margarine
I egg, beaten
beaten egg, to glaze (optional)

1 To make the yeast batter using dried yeast, place the yeast and sugar in a small jug. Stir in the milk and leave for 5 minutes.

2 Stir in the flour and leave in a warm place until frothy (about 15–20 minutes).

3 To make the yeast batter using fresh yeast, place the yeast, sugar and milk in a small jug. Stir in the flour and leave in a warm place until frothy (about 15–20 minutes).

4 In a large bowl, sift together the flour and salt and mix in the sugar. Rub in the margarine. Stir in the egg and the yeast batter and mix to give a soft dough.

5 Turn on to a floured surface and knead for 8–10 minutes, until the dough is smooth, elastic and no longer sticky.

6 Oil or grease a 450 g (1 lb) loaf tin. Press the dough out and shape to fit the tin. Cover the tin with an oiled polythene bag and leave to rise in a warm place for about 1 hour, until doubled in size.

7 Preheat the oven to Gas Mark 7/electric oven 220°C/fan oven 200°C.

8 Before baking, dust the top of the loaf with flour for a soft crust or brush with beaten egg for a shiny crust.

9 Bake for 30–40 minutes, until the loaf is golden and the base sounds hollow when tapped. Transfer to a wire rack to cool.

MAKES 4 naan breads
PREPARATION TIME:
10–15 minutes + rising
COOKING TIME: 10–15 minutes
FREEZING: recommended

Naan is the Persian word for bread and is commonly used in India and many Asian countries. These are flat breads with a crisp crust usually served with Indian meals.

300 g (11 oz) strong white flour
1 teaspoon salt
1 teaspoon baking powder
1½ teaspoons easy-blend yeast
3 tablespoons natural yogurt
1½ tablespoons sunflower oil
150 ml (¼ pint) hand-hot water

1 Sift together the flour, salt and baking powder into a mixing bowl.
2 Stir in the yeast. Add the yogurt, oil and water to form a soft dough.
3 Knead until smooth and elastic.
4 Place in a clean, greased bowl, cover and leave to rise until doubled in size.
5 Knock back, divide the dough into four and roll each piece into an oval 20 by 15 cm (8 by 6 inches). Leave to prove for 15 minutes.
6 Preheat the grill until very hot and cook the breads under the grill for 3–4 minutes on each side, or until golden and puffy.

NAAN

MAKES a 900 g (2 lb) loaf
PREPARATION TIME: 10–15 minutes
COOKING TIME: 25–35 minutes
FREEZING: recommended

MAKES 1 loaf
PREPARATION TIME: 10–15 minutes + rising
COOKING TIME: 25–30 minutes
FREEZING: recommended

SODA BREAD

GLUTEN-FREE BREAD

A traditional recipe from Ireland. Whenever I visit my sister-in-law's family there's always this freshly made bread that can be served with smoked salmon or soups to make a substantial lunch. Children and adults alike enjoy this bread. It's also a good bread for those with a yeast intolerance.

675 g (1½ lb) strong wholemeal flour
225 g (8 oz) strong white flour
2 teaspoons salt
2 teaspoons bicarbonate of soda
4 teaspoons cream of tartar
2 teaspoons caster sugar
50 g (2 oz) butter
575–850 ml (1–1½ pints) hand-hot milk

1 Preheat the oven to Gas Mark 5/electric oven 190°C/fan oven 170°C.
2 Sift the dry ingredients into a large bowl.
3 Rub in the butter and mix to a soft dough with the milk.
4 Shape into a large circle about 2.5 cm (1-inch) thick on a floured surface, with the minimum amount of kneading.
5 Place on a greased baking tray and make a cross in the top of the loaf.
6 Bake for 25–35 minutes until well risen and golden in colour. As soda bread has a dense texture it won't sound hollow when it is knocked.
7 Transfer to a wire rack to cool.

This is a recipe I frequently use when entertaining friends on gluten-free diets and it's often happily eaten by others as well.

300 g (11 oz) gluten-free flour
80 g (3 oz) ground almonds
1 teaspoon salt
1½ teaspoons sugar
2 teaspoons easy-blend yeast
150 ml (¼ pint) hand-hot milk
175 ml (6 fl oz) hand-hot water
beaten egg, to glaze (optional)

1 Mix together the flour, almonds, salt, sugar and yeast in a mixing bowl.
2 Beat in the milk and water to form a batter.
3 Pour into a 900 g (2 lb) greased loaf tin and leave to rise for 30 minutes.
4 Preheat the oven to Gas Mark 7/electric oven 220°C/fan oven 200°C.
5 Bake for 25–30 minutes. If you like, brush the loaf with beaten egg after 20 minutes for a more golden appearance. Transfer to a wire rack to cool.

MAKES 1 plait
PREPARATION TIME: 25–30 minutes + rising
COOKING TIME: 20–30 minutes
FREEZING: recommended

MAKES a 450 g (1 lb) loaf
PREPARATION TIME: 15–20 minutes + rising
COOKING TIME: 20–30 minutes
FREEZING: recommended

OAT PLAIT

POTATO BREAD

The rolled oats give a crunchy texture to this bread. Eat slices of this loaf with creamy soft cheese.

350 g (12 oz) strong brown flour
1 teaspoon salt
115 g (4 oz) rolled oats
1 sachet easy-blend yeast
2 tablespoons olive oil
150 ml (¼ pint) hand-hot water
150 ml (¼ pint) hand-hot milk

1 Into a large bowl, sift the flour and salt and then add the oats and yeast.
2 Stir in the oil and enough water and milk to form a soft dough.
3 Turn on to a lightly floured surface and knead until smooth and elastic.
4 Place in a clean, greased bowl, cover and leave to rise in a warm place until doubled in size.
5 Knock back and knead again.
6 Divide the dough into three equal pieces, roll into three sausages of about 30 cm (12 inches) long and plait them together. Dampen the ends with water, pinch them together and tuck them under slightly to finish the loaf neatly.
7 Place on a greased baking tray. Cover and prove for 25–35 minutes, until doubled in size.
8 Preheat the oven to Gas Mark 6/electric oven 200°C/fan oven 180°C.
9 Brush with milk and sprinkle with a few extra oats. Bake for 20–30 minutes. The base will sound hollow when knocked. Transfer to a wire rack to cool.

The potato gives this bread a moister texture and the addition of sage enhances the flavour.

300 g (11 oz) strong white flour
½ teaspoon salt
1 teaspoon easy-blend yeast
80 g (3 oz) cooked, mashed potatoes
1 tablespoon chopped fresh sage (optional)
80 g (3 oz) butter, melted and cooled
1 egg
75–100 ml (2½–3½ fl oz) milk.

1 Sift the flour and salt into a mixing bowl. Add the yeast. Stir in the mashed potato, sage (if using), butter and egg. Stir in enough milk to form a soft dough.
2 Knead the dough until smooth and elastic.
3 Shape to fit a 450 g (1 lb) greased loaf tin. Leave to rise until doubled in size.
4 Preheat the oven to Gas Mark 7/electric oven 220°C/fan oven 200°C.
5 Bake for 20–30 minutes, until well risen and golden brown. Transfer to a wire rack to cool.

MAKES a 900 g (2 lb) loaf
PREPARATION TIME: 20–25 minutes + rising
COOKING TIME: 30–40 minutes
FREEZING: recommended

The different flavours and textures of the sunflower, pumpkin and sesame seeds give this bread a **distinctive taste**.

THREE-SEED LOAF

450 g (1 lb) strong brown flour
225 g (8 oz) strong white flour
2 teaspoons salt
25 g (1 oz) butter
50 g (2 oz) sunflower seeds
25 g (1 oz) pumpkin seeds
1 sachet easy-blend dried yeast
450 ml (16 fl oz) hand-hot water
1 tablespoon sesame seeds

1 Into a bowl, sift the flours and salt. Cut the butter into small pieces and rub into the flour, until it resembles fine breadcrumbs. Stir in the sunflower and pumpkin seeds.
2 Mix in the yeast and gradually stir in the liquid, mixing to form a rough ball.
3 Using your hands, draw the mixture together into a ball. Turn on to a floured surface.
4 Knead the dough for 8–10 minutes, until the dough is smooth, elastic and no longer sticky.
5 Oil or grease a 900 g (2 lb) loaf tin. Press the dough out and shape to fit the tin. Cover the tin with an oiled polythene bag and leave to rise in a warm place for about 1 hour, until doubled in size.

6 Preheat the oven to Gas Mark 7/electric oven 220°C/fan oven 200°C.
7 Before baking, brush the top with a little water and sprinkle with the sesame seeds.
8 Bake for 30–40 minutes, until the loaf is golden and the base sounds hollow when tapped.
9 Transfer to a wire rack to cool.

Savoury breads can be made using white, brown or wholemeal flours, along with other ingredients such as cheeses, onion, herbs, and seeds. The increased availability of ingredients such as sun-dried tomatoes, olives, basil and feta cheese makes bread-making all the more interesting, and experimentation with flavouring

SAVOURY BREADS

all the more rewarding. There are heady, Mediterranean flavours and aromas here, as in Sun-dried Tomato and Olive Plait and Feta Cheese and Sage Cottage Loaf. The interesting shapes and flavours make these breads particularly good to serve with lunches and salads.

MAKES 1 round loaf
PREPARATION TIME: 15–20 minutes
COOKING TIME: 35–45 minutes
FREEZING: recommended

The addition of Greece's best-known cheese combines well with the sage and onion flavours. This loaf uses self-raising flour and doesn't need any other raising agent and can just be mixed, without kneading, rising or proving. The finished loaf has a **rustic appeal** and will add interest to any buffet table.

175 g (6 oz) self-raising flour
1 teaspoon salt
a pinch of cayenne pepper
4–5 spring onions, sliced finely
1 teaspoon chopped fresh sage
115 g (4 oz) feta cheese, cubed
1 potato, weighing about 175 g (6 oz)
1 egg
2–3 tablespoons milk
1 teaspoon mustard

1 Preheat the oven to Gas Mark 5/electric oven 190°C/fan oven 170°C. Sift the flour, salt and cayenne pepper together.
2 Stir in the spring onions, sage and two-thirds of the cheese.
3 Peel the potato and coarsely grate it into the mixture. Stir until the potato flakes are coated with the flour.
4 Mix together the egg, milk and mustard. Pour into the mixture and mix to form a rough dough.
5 Place on a greased baking tray and form into a 15 cm (6-inch) round. Press the remaining feta cheese over the surface and dust lightly with flour.
6 Bake in the preheated oven for 35–45 minutes, until the loaf is golden brown.
7 Transfer to a wire rack to cool. Serve warm.

FETA CHEESE & SAGE COTTAGE LOAF

MAKES 1 oval loaf
PREPARATION TIME:
15–20 minutes + rising
COOKING TIME: 20–25 minutes
FREEZING: recommended

An Italian bread with a light texture, ciabatta is delicious served with cold poached salmon and salad or used as a base for pizzas, as described on page 23.

SUNFLOWER CIABATTA

250 g (9 oz) strong white flour
½ teaspoon salt
1 teaspoon easy-blend yeast
1 teaspoon sugar
25 g (1 oz) sunflower seeds
1½ tablespoons olive oil
175 ml (6 fl oz) hand-hot water

1 Sift the flour and salt into a bowl. Add the yeast, sugar and sunflower seeds.
2 Add the oil and enough water to form a soft dough.
3 Turn on to a lightly floured surface and knead until smooth.
4 Place in a clean, greased bowl, cover and leave to rise until doubled in size.
5 Knock back and shape into an oval.

6 Place on a greased baking tray and leave to prove for 30 minutes.
7 Preheat the oven to Gas Mark 7/electric oven 220°C/fan oven 200°C.
8 Bake the loaf for 20–25 minutes or until golden and the base sounds hollow when tapped. Transfer to a wire rack to cool.

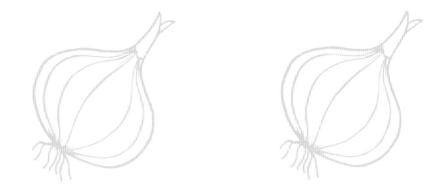

MAKES 1 ring
PREPARATION TIME:
15–20 minutes + rising
COOKING TIME: 25–30 minutes
FREEZING: recommended

A well flavoured bread that is **delicious** with cheese and salad.

CHEESE & ONION LOAF

15 g (½ oz) fresh yeast or 1 sachet of easy-blend yeast
1 teaspoon caster sugar
15 g (½ oz) ascorbic acid (if using fresh yeast)
200–250 ml (7–9 fl oz) hand-hot water
2 tablespoons sunflower oil
1 small onion, chopped
375 g (13 oz) strong white flour
1 teaspoon salt
1 teaspoon mustard powder
50 g (2 oz) Cheddar cheese, grated
beaten egg, for brushing
poppy seeds, to decorate

1 For fresh yeast, blend the yeast, sugar, ascorbic acid and half the water together. Leave until frothy. Add the remaining water and a tablespoon of the oil.

2 Meanwhile, heat the remaining oil in a small pan and cook the onion until soft but not browned.

3 Sift the flour into a bowl. Add the salt, mustard powder, cheese and onion. If using easy-blend yeast, mix it and the sugar with the flour now.

4 Add the yeast liquid if using fresh yeast, or just the water and oil and mix to form a soft dough.

5 Turn on to a lightly floured surface and knead until smooth.

6 Divide the mixture in half. Roll one half into a circle and place on a greased, loose-based tin.

7 Divide the remaining dough into six and form into rolls. Place the rolls on top of the circle. Cover and leave to rise until doubled in size.

8 Preheat the oven to Gas Mark 7/electric oven 220°C/fan oven 200°C.

9 Brush with egg and sprinkle with poppy seeds. Bake in the preheated oven for 25–30 minutes until golden and hollow-sounding when the base is tapped.

10 Remove from the tin and transfer to a wire rack to cool.

MAKES 4 individual pizzas
PREPARATION TIME: 20–25 minutes + rising
COOKING TIME: 20–30 minutes
FREEZING: recommended

CALZONE PIZZAS

In case you've never seen these made, they are like a folded over pizza. These make an ideal lunch served with a salad – **a meal in an edible packet!**

FOR THE DOUGH:
450 g (1 lb) strong white flour
½ teaspoon salt
50 g (2 oz) margarine
½ sachet easy-blend yeast
1 teaspoon caster sugar
1 egg
200 ml (7 fl oz) hand-hot milk

FOR THE FILLING:
25 g (1 oz) butter
1 large onion, chopped finely
½ teaspoon dried oregano
200 g (7 oz) canned tomatoes
2 tablespoons tomato purée
80 g (3 oz) sliced button mushrooms
80 g (3 oz) cooked ham, chopped
150 g (5 oz) mozzarella cheese, grated
salt and freshly ground pepper
beaten egg, to glaze

TO MAKE THE DOUGH
1 Sift the flour and salt into a bowl. Rub in the margarine until the mixture resembles fine breadcrumbs.
2 Stir in the yeast and sugar. Add the egg and milk and mix to form a soft dough.
3 Turn the dough on to a floured surface and knead well until the dough is smooth and elastic.
4 Place the dough in a clean, greased bowl, cover and leave to rise until doubled in size.

TO MAKE THE FILLING
1 Melt the butter in a saucepan, add the onion, oregano and seasoning. Cook gently until the onion is tender.
2 Stir in the tomatoes and tomato purée. Bring to the boil and cook rapidly until the mixture is thick. Leave to cool. Preheat the oven to Gas Mark 6/electric oven 200°C/fan oven 180°C.

TO ASSEMBLE AND BAKE THE PIZZAS
1 When the dough has risen, knock it back and cut into four equal pieces. Roll each piece into a 20 cm (8-inch) round.
2 Spread 1 tablespoon of tomato mixture over half of each dough round. Cover with one quarter of the sliced mushrooms and chopped ham. Sprinkle 25 g (1 oz) of cheese on each round.
3 Brush the edges of the dough with water. Fold the plain half of the dough over the filling and press the edges together. Ensure the edges are well sealed and brush each pizza with beaten egg and sprinkle on the remaining cheese.
4 Place on a greased baking tray. Bake in the preheated oven for 20–30 minutes.
5 Make the remaining tomato mixture into a sauce by adding 300 ml (½ pint) of water and then puréeing in a blender.
6 Serve the pizzas with warmed sauce.

MAKES 1 round loaf
PREPARATION TIME: 15–20 minutes + rising
COOKING TIME: 20–25 minutes
FREEZING: recommended

SUN-DRIED TOMATO, OLIVE & BASIL FOCCACIA

A traditional flat bread from the northern

shores of the Mediterranean.

350 g (12 oz) strong white flour
1½ teaspoons salt
1 sachet of easy-blend yeast
8 sun-dried tomatoes, chopped
12 stoned olives, halved
8 fresh basil leaves, chopped roughly
200 ml (7 fl oz) hand-hot water
5–6 tablespoons extra-virgin olive oil

1 Sift the flour and salt into a large bowl. Add the yeast, tomatoes, half the olives and most of the basil.
2 Gradually stir in the water and 3 tablespoons of the olive oil to make a soft dough.
3 Turn on to a floured surface and knead the dough until smooth and elastic.
4 Shape into a 25 cm (10-inch) round, place on a greased baking tray and prick all over with a fork. Cover with greased clingfilm and leave in a warm place until doubled in size.
5 Preheat the oven to Gas Mark 7/electric oven 220°C/fan oven 200°C.
6 When risen, remove the clingfilm and gently press the remaining olives into the dough.
7 Trickle the rest of the olive oil over the dough, spreading it lightly with your fingers. Sprinkle over the rest of the basil and a little salt.
8 Bake in the preheated oven for 20–25 minutes, until golden and hollow-sounding when the base is tapped. Transfer to a wire rack to cool.

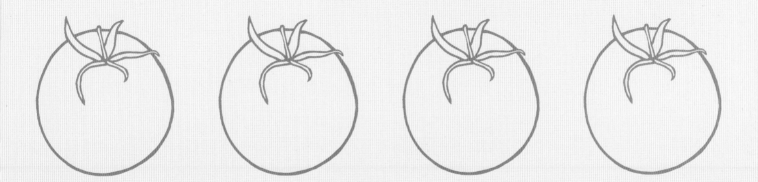

MAKES 1 plait
PREPARATION TIME: 20 minutes + rising
COOKING TIME: 30–35 minutes
FREEZING: recommended

I first started making this bread when sun-dried tomatoes became readily available in this country. The mix of the sun-dried tomatoes and olives gives this a Mediterranean influence when entertaining outside on a **summer's day**.

450 g (1 lb) strong brown flour
1 teaspoon salt
25 g (1 oz) butter
1 sachet easy-blend dried yeast
50 g (2 oz) sun-dried tomatoes chopped
25 g (1 oz) stoned black olives, sliced
300 ml (10 fl oz) hand-hot water

1 In a bowl, sift the flour and salt. Cut the butter into small pieces and rub into the flour until it resembles fine breadcrumbs.
2 Mix in the yeast, tomatoes and olives. Gradually stir in the liquid, mixing to form a rough ball.
3 Using your hands, draw the mixture together into a ball. Turn on to a floured surface.
4 Knead the dough for 8–10 minutes until the dough is smooth, elastic and no longer sticky.
5 Place in a clean, greased bowl and cover. Leave to rise until doubled in size.
6 Knock back and knead.
7 Divide the dough into three equal pieces. Roll each into a sausage about 30 cm (12 inches) wide and plait them together.
8 Place on a greased baking tray. Cover and prove for 25–35 minutes until doubled in size.
9 Preheat the oven to Gas Mark 7/electric oven 220°C/fan oven 200°C.
10 Bake in the preheated oven, for 30–35 minutes, until the loaf is golden and the base sounds hollow when tapped. Transfer to a wire rack to cool.

SUN-DRIED TOMATO & OLIVE PLAIT

Sweet breads contain sugar and different fruits and nuts to give them flavour – traditionally currants, raisins and sultanas are used. In this chapter there are also recipes that include more exotic dried fruit, such as papaya, mango and pineapple. Coconut milk gives an interesting combination when used with lime in Coconut and Lime

SWEET BREADS

Loaf and there's even a bread for chocoholics. If you are after something a bit unusual why not try the Fruit Pizza here. The tangy fruit and the soft pizza base are a delicious combination. Both this recipe and the Sweet Naan with Cherries and Almonds make great teatime treats.

MAKES a 900 g (2 lb) loaf
PREPARATION TIME: 25–30 minutes
+ activating yeast + rising
COOKING TIME: 25–35 minutes
FREEZING: recommended

A traditional fruit bread that tastes equally good toasted,

with lots of butter.

FRUIT LOAF

150 ml (¼ pint) hand-hot water
150 ml (¼ pint) hand-hot milk
1 teaspoon + 25 g (1 oz) caster sugar
15 g (½ oz) dried yeast
450 g (1 lb) strong white flour
1 teaspoon salt
25 g (1 oz) margarine
175 g (6 oz) mixed dried fruit

1 Mix together the water and milk and dissolve the teaspoon of sugar in the liquid. Sprinkle in the yeast and stir to mix. Leave in a warm place for 10–15 minutes, until frothy.

2 Sift the flour and salt into a bowl, rub in the margarine and add the 25 g (1 oz) of caster sugar. Stir in the dried fruit. Add the yeast mixture and mix to form a soft dough.

3 Knead the dough on a floured surface until smooth and elastic. Place in a clean, greased bowl, cover and leave to rise until doubled in size.

4 Turn the dough on to a floured surface, knock back and knead.

5 Shape to fit a 900 g (2 lb) greased loaf tin. Cover and leave to prove for 30 minutes.

6 Preheat the oven to Gas Mark 6/electric oven 200°C/fan oven 180°C.

7 Bake the loaf for 25–35 minutes, until golden and hollow-sounding when tapped on the base. Transfer to a wire rack to cool.

MAKES a 900 g (2 lb) loaf
PREPARATION TIME: 20–25 minutes + rising
COOKING TIME: 25–35 minutes
FREEZING: recommended

BRAZIL NUT & APRICOT BREAD

The combination of fruit and nuts gives this light bread a delicious taste.

450 g (1 lb) strong white flour
1 teaspoon salt
25 g (1 oz) margarine
25 g (1 oz) caster sugar
1 teaspoon easy-blend yeast
115 g (4 oz) ready-to-eat dried apricots, chopped
80 g (3 oz) brazil nuts, chopped roughly
150 ml (1/4 pint) hand-hot water
150 ml (1/4 pint) hand-hot milk

1 Sift the flour and salt into a bowl and rub in the margarine until the mixture resembles fine breadcrumbs.
2 Add the caster sugar and yeast. Stir in the apricots and nuts. Add enough liquid to form a soft dough.
3 Knead the dough on a floured surface until smooth and elastic.
4 Place in a clean greased bowl, cover and leave to rise until doubled in size.
5 Turn the dough on to a floured surface, knock back and knead.
6 Shape to fit a 900 g (2 lb) greased loaf tin, cover and leave to prove for 30 minutes.
7 Preheat the oven to Gas Mark 6/electric oven 200°C/fan oven 180°C.
8 Bake for 25–35 minutes, until golden and hollow-sounding when tapped on the base. Transfer to a wire rack to cool.

MAKES a 450 g (1 lb) loaf
PREPARATION TIME: 10–15 minutes + rising
COOKING TIME: 20–25 minutes
FREEZING: recommended

CHOCOLATE BREAD

Plain, milk or white chocolate chips can be used in this sweet loaf, which is delicious eaten with a red berry jam.

225 g (8 oz) strong white flour
1 tablespoon cocoa powder
1/2 teaspoon salt
1 teaspoon easy-blend yeast
25 g (1 oz) margarine
25 g (1 oz) caster sugar
50 g chocolate chips
1 egg
125 ml (41/2 fl oz) hand-hot milk

1 In a large bowl, sift together the flour, cocoa powder and salt. Add the yeast. Rub in the margarine. Stir in the sugar and chocolate chips. Stir in the egg and milk, mixing to give a soft dough.
2 Turn on to a floured surface and knead for 8–10 minutes, until the dough is smooth, elastic and no longer sticky.
3 Oil or grease a 450 g (1 lb) loaf tin. Press the dough out and shape to fit the tin. Cover the tin with an oiled polythene bag and leave to rise in a warm place for about 1 hour, until doubled in size.
4 Preheat the oven to Gas Mark 7/electric oven 220°C/fan oven 200°C.
5 Bake for 20–25 minutes, until the loaf is golden and the base sounds hollow when tapped.
6 Transfer to a wire rack to cool.

MAKES a 450 g (1 lb) loaf
PREPARATION TIME: 20–25 minutes + activating yeast + rising
COOKING TIME: 30–40 minutes
FREEZING: recommended

CURRANT LOAF

Currants are a small black variety of dried grape, first grown in Corinth in Greece. They now come from Australia and the USA as well.

FOR THE YEAST BATTER:

2 teaspoons dried yeast or 15 g (½ oz) fresh yeast
½ teaspoon caster sugar
5 tablespoons hand-hot milk
50 g (2 oz) strong white flour

FOR THE DOUGH:

175 g (6 oz) strong white flour
½ teaspoon salt
25 g (1 oz) caster sugar
25 g (1 oz) margarine
175 g (6 oz) currants
1 egg, beaten

1 To make the yeast batter using dried yeast, place the yeast and sugar in a small jug. Stir in the milk and leave for 5 minutes.
2 Stir in the flour and leave in a warm place until frothy (about 15–20 minutes).
3 To make the yeast batter using fresh yeast, place the yeast, sugar and milk in a small jug. Stir in the flour and leave in a warm place until frothy (about 15–20 minutes).
4 In a large bowl, sift together the flour and salt and mix in the sugar. Rub in the margarine and add the currants. Stir in the egg and the yeast batter and mix to give a soft dough.
5 Turn on to a floured surface and knead for 8–10 minutes, until the dough is smooth, elastic and no longer sticky.
6 Oil or grease a 450 g (1 lb) loaf tin. Press the dough out and shape to fit the tin. Cover the tin with an oiled polythene bag and leave to rise in a warm place for about 1 hour, until doubled in size.
7 Preheat the oven to Gas Mark 7/electric oven 220°C/fan oven 200°C.
8 Bake in the preheated oven for 30–40 minutes, until the loaf is golden and the base sounds hollow when tapped. Transfer to a wire rack to cool.

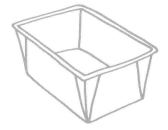
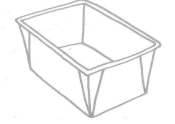
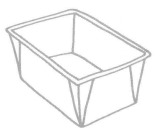

MAKES a 30 cm (12-inch) pizza
PREPARATION TIME:
20–25 minutes + rising
COOKING TIME: 20–30 minutes
FREEZING: recommended (base only)

This fun dessert makes a change from a savoury version. It evolved from having a quantity of fruit left over following a food photography session. The fruits can be varied according to the season.

225 g (8 oz) strong white flour
½ teaspoon salt
25 g (1 oz) margarine
½ sachet easy-blend yeast
1 teaspoon caster sugar
1 egg
115 ml (4 fl oz) hand-hot milk

FOR THE TOPPING:
6 tablespoons apricot jam, warmed
1 peach, sliced
115 g (4 oz) strawberries, sliced
1 orange, sliced in circles
1 kiwi fruit, sliced
2 tablespoons icing sugar, sifted

1 Sift the flour and salt into a bowl. Rub in the margarine until the mixture resembles fine breadcrumbs. Stir in the yeast and sugar. Add the egg and milk and mix to form a soft dough.
2 Turn the dough on to a floured surface and knead well until the dough is smooth and elastic.
3 Place the dough in a clean, greased bowl, cover and leave to rise until doubled in size.
4 Preheat the oven to Gas Mark 6/electric oven 200°C/fan oven 180°C.
5 When the dough has risen, knock it back. Roll into a 30 cm (12-inch) round and place on a greased baking tray. Bake for 10 minutes.
6 Remove from the oven, spread with apricot jam and place the fruit on top. Continue cooking for a further 15 minutes. Sprinkle with icing sugar in the last 5 minutes for a glazed finish.

FRUIT PIZZA

MAKES 4 naans
PREPARATION TIME: 15–20 minutes + rising
COOKING TIME: 10–15 minutes
FREEZING: recommended

MAKES a 450 g (1 lb) loaf
PREPARATION TIME: 25–30 minutes + rising
COOKING TIME: 25–30 minutes
FREEZING: recommended

SWEET NAAN WITH CHERRIES AND ALMONDS

A SWEET GLUTEN-FREE LOAF

Traditionally naan is cooked in a clay oven called a tandoor. This sweet version is cooked under a hot grill.

675 g (1½ lb) strong white flour

1 teaspoon salt

2 teaspoons baking powder

1 sachet easy-blend yeast

115 ml (4 fl oz) natural yogurt

1 tablespoon oil

350 ml (12 fl oz) hand-hot water

25 g (1 oz) unsalted butter, softened

25 g (1 oz) desiccated coconut

115 g (4 oz) glacé cherries, chopped

25 g (1 oz) ground almonds

1 Sift the flour, salt and baking powder into a mixing bowl. Stir in the yeast. Add the yogurt, oil and enough water to form a soft dough.
2 Knead until smooth and elastic.
3 Place in a clean, greased bowl and leave to rise until doubled in size.
4 Knock back, divide the dough into four and roll each piece into an oval 20 by 15 cm (8 by 6 inches).
5 Spread each with a little butter and press the coconut, cherries and ground almonds on to the surface. Fold in half and re-roll to the original size.
6 Leave to prove for 15 minutes.
7 Preheat the grill and cook under a hot grill for 3–4 minutes on each side, until golden and puffy.

My sister-in-law and several friends are coeliacs (have a gluten intolerance). I first made this bread as an alternative at tea-time as they often complained about having to exclude everyday foods from their diets. Since then many of them have begun to make it themselves.

grated zest and juice of 1 orange

80 g (3 oz) stoned dates, chopped

300 g (11 oz) gluten-free flour

80 g (3 oz) ground almonds

1 teaspoon salt

25 g (1 oz) caster sugar

2 teaspoons easy-blend yeast

150 ml (¼ pint) hand-hot milk

175 ml (6 fl oz) hand-hot water

1 tablespoon flaked almonds

1 Heat the orange juice in a small saucepan. Add the zest and chopped dates. Leave to stand, off the heat, for 15 minutes.
2 Purée the mixture.
3 Mix together flour, almonds, salt, sugar and yeast in a mixing bowl. Beat in the date purée, milk and water to form a batter.
4 Pour into a 900 g (2 lb) greased loaf tin. Leave to rise, uncovered, for 30 minutes.
5 Preheat the oven to Gas Mark 7/electric oven 220°C/fan oven 200°C.
6 Bake for 25–30 minutes. After 20 minutes, sprinkle the almonds over the top and continue cooking until a skewer inserted in the centre of the loaf comes out clean.

MAKES a 450 g (1 lb) loaf
PREPARATION TIME: 10–15 minutes + rising
COOKING TIME: 20–25 minutes
FREEZING: recommended

TROPICAL LOAF WITH PAPAYA, MANGO & PINEAPPLE

A delicious soft bread with chunks of exotic

dried fruit throughout.

225 g (8 oz) strong white flour
1 teaspoon easy-blend yeast
½ teaspoon salt
25 g (1 oz) margarine
50 g (2 oz) ready-to-eat dried papaya, chopped
50 g (2 oz) ready-to-eat dried mango, chopped
50 g (2 oz) ready-to-eat dried pineapple, chopped
25 g (1 oz) caster sugar
1 egg, beaten
125 ml (4½ fl oz) hand-hot milk

1 In a large bowl, sift together the flour, yeast and salt. Rub in the margarine. Stir in the chopped fruits and sugar. Stir in the egg and enough milk to give a soft dough.
2 Turn on to a floured surface and knead for 8–10 minutes, until the dough is smooth, elastic and no longer sticky.
3 Oil or grease a 450 g (1 lb) loaf tin. Press the dough out and shape to fit the tin. Cover the tin with an oiled polythene bag and leave to rise in a warm place for about 1 hour until doubled in size.
4 Preheat the oven to Gas Mark 7/electric oven 220°C/fan oven 200°C.
5 Bake for 20–25 minutes, until the loaf is golden and the base sounds hollow when tapped.
6 Transfer to a wire rack to cool.

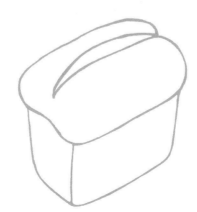

MAKES a 450 g (1 lb) loaf
PREPARATION TIME: 15–20 minutes
+ rising
COOKING TIME: 25–30 minutes
FREEZING: recommended

When experimenting with the ice-cream maker last summer I ended up with an opened tin of coconut milk and limes left over, so this bread came into being. The **exotic combination of flavours** makes it ideal for breakfast or a summer tea.

225 g (8 oz) strong white flour
1 teaspoon easy-blend yeast
½ teaspoon salt
25 g (1 oz) margarine
grated zest of 1 lime
25 g (1 oz) caster sugar
1 egg, beaten
125 ml (4½ fl oz) coconut milk

1 In a large bowl, sift together the flour, yeast and salt. Rub in the margarine until the mixture resembles fine breadcrumbs. Stir in the lime zest and sugar. Stir in the egg and coconut milk, mixing to give a soft dough.
2 Turn on to a floured surface and knead for 8–10 minutes, until the dough is smooth, elastic and no longer sticky.
3 Oil or grease a 450 g (1 lb) loaf tin. Press the dough out and shape to fit the tin. Cover the tin with an oiled polythene bag and leave to rise in a warm place for about 1 hour, until doubled in size.
4 Preheat the oven to Gas Mark 6/electric oven 210°C/fan oven 190°C.
5 Bake for 25–30 minutes, until the loaf is golden and the base sounds hollow when tapped.
6 Transfer to a wire rack to cool.

COCONUT & LIME LOAF

In this chapter, eggs, milk and butter, along with other ingredients, are added to bread doughs to enrich their flavour and give them a special texture. Some of these recipes are regional classics, while others are based on traditional ideas but are updated, for example Savoury Whirls with Tomato and Basil are a form of savoury

ENRICHED BREADS

'Chelsea bun'. In some cases the fat is added to the dough by rolling and folding, which produces a delicious, flaky finish when baked – Olive and Cheese Bread Ring, Croissants and Fraserburgh Rolls are all examples of this technique.

MAKES 9 buns
PREPARATION TIME: 30–35 minutes
+ activating yeast + rising
COOKING TIME: 25–30 minutes
FREEZING: recommended

A traditional recipe for this sweet bun. A real old
English favourite.

CHELSEA BUNS

FOR THE YEAST BATTER:
2 teaspoons dried yeast or 15 g (½ oz)
fresh yeast
½ teaspoon caster sugar
5 tablespoons hand-hot milk
50 g (2 oz) strong white flour

FOR THE DOUGH:
175 g (6 oz) strong white flour
½ teaspoon salt
25 g (1 oz) caster sugar
25 g (1 oz) margarine
1 egg, beaten

FOR THE FILLING:
25 g (1 oz) butter, melted
115 g (4 oz) mixed dried fruit
50 g (2 oz) dark brown sugar
½ teaspoon ground cinnamon

1 To make the yeast batter using dried yeast, place the yeast and sugar in a small jug. Stir in the milk and leave for 5 minutes.
2 Stir in the flour and leave in a warm place until frothy (about 15–20 minutes).
3 Alternatively, to make the yeast batter using fresh yeast, place the yeast, sugar and milk in a small jug. Stir in the flour and leave in a warm place until frothy (about 15–20 minutes).
4 In a large bowl, sift together the flour and salt and mix in the sugar. Rub in the margarine. Stir in the egg and the yeast batter and mix to give a soft dough.
5 Turn on to a floured surface and knead for 8–10 minutes, until the dough is smooth, elastic and no longer sticky. Place the dough in a clean, greased bowl, cover and leave to rise until doubled in size.
6 Transfer the risen dough to a lightly floured surface. Knock back and knead. Roll the dough into a rectangle 30 by 23 cm (12 by 9 inches). Brush the surface with the melted butter. Sprinkle with the fruit, sugar and cinnamon.
7 Roll up the dough like a swiss roll, starting at the longest side.
8 Cut into nine equal pieces and place on a greased baking tray, cut-side down, to form a square, about 1 cm (½ inch) apart. Cover and leave to prove for about 30 minutes until well risen.
9 Preheat the oven to Gas Mark 7/electric oven 220°C/fan oven 200°C.
10 Bake for 25–30 minutes, until golden brown. Place on a wire rack to cool

MAKES a 20 cm (8-inch) round
PREPARATION TIME:
10–15 minutes + rising
COOKING TIME: 20–25 minutes

A round tea cake traditionally split, toasted and buttered, re-assembled and sliced for serving.

200 ml (7 fl oz) milk
25 g (1 oz) butter
350 g (12 oz) strong white flour
½ teaspoon salt
1 teaspoon easy-blend yeast
1 teaspoon sugar
1 egg

FOR THE GLAZE:
1 tablespoon granulated sugar
1 tablespoon milk

1   Heat the milk gently in a small pan, add the butter and allow to melt. Cool the mixture so that it is hand-hot.
2   Sift the flour and salt into a mixing bowl and add the yeast and sugar.
3   Beat the egg and add to the milk mixture.
4   Stir the egg mixture into the flour to form a soft dough. Turn on to a floured surface and knead until smooth and elastic.
5   Shape and place in a greased 20 cm (8-inch) round cake tin. Leave to prove until doubled in size.
6   Preheat the oven to Gas Mark 7/electric oven 220°C/fan oven 200°C.
7   Bake for 20–25 minutes.
8   To glaze, mix together the sugar and milk and brush the top of the bread with this in the last 5 minutes of cooking. Remove from the tin and transfer to a wire rack to cool.

SALLY LUNN

MAKES a 450 g (1 lb) loaf
PREPARATION TIME:
30–35 minutes + rising
COOKING TIME: 25–30 minutes
FREEZING: recommended

Having spent many holidays visiting America, I noticed that cinnamon and raisins were found in many delicious American breakfast foods; this bread is lovely toasted, with maple syrup drizzled over it.

225 g (8 oz) strong white flour
½ teaspoon salt
25 g (1 oz) caster sugar
25 g (1 oz) margarine
½ sachet easy-blend yeast
1 egg, beaten
5 tablespoons hand-hot milk
grated zest and juice of ½ orange
1 tablespoon ground cinnamon
25 g (1 oz) dark brown sugar

1 In a large bowl, sift together the flour and salt and then mix in the sugar. Rub in the margarine and add the yeast. Stir in the egg and milk to give a soft dough.
2 Turn on to a floured surface and knead for 8–10 minutes, until the dough is smooth, elastic and no longer sticky.
3 Place the dough in a clean, greased bowl, cover and leave to rise until doubled in size
4 Transfer the risen dough to a lightly floured surface. Knock back and knead in the orange, cinnamon and sugar until evenly distributed.
5 Roll the dough into a rectangle 33 by 15 cm (13 by 6 inches). Roll up tightly and place in a greased 450 g (1 lb) loaf tin. Cover and prove until doubled in size.
6 Preheat the oven to Gas Mark 6/electric oven 200°C/fan oven 180°C.
7 Bake for 25–30 minutes, until golden brown. Place on a wire rack to cool.

CINNAMON & RAISIN SWIRL

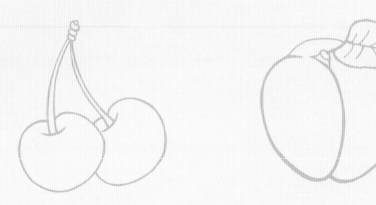

MAKES 9 buns
PREPARATION TIME: 25–30 minutes + rising
COOKING TIME: 25–30 minutes
FREEZING: recommended

These are made in a similar way to Chelsea Buns, and have a fresh, crunchy taste and texture.

225 g (8 oz) strong white flour
½ teaspoon salt
25 g (1 oz) caster sugar
25 g (1 oz) margarine
½ sachet easy-blend yeast
1 egg, beaten
5 tablespoons hand-hot milk

FOR THE FILLING:
25 g (1 oz) butter
50 g (2 oz) dark brown sugar
50 g (2 oz) walnuts
25 g (1 oz) dried apricots, chopped
25 g (1 oz) glacé cherries, chopped

1 In a large bowl, sift together the flour and salt and mix in the sugar. Rub in the margarine and add the yeast. Stir in the egg and milk to give a soft dough.
2 Turn on to a floured surface and knead for 8–10 minutes, until the dough is smooth, elastic and no longer sticky. Place the dough in a clean, greased bowl, cover and leave to rise until doubled in size.
3 Transfer the risen dough to a lightly floured surface. Knock back and knead. Roll the dough into a rectangle 30 by 23 cm (12 by 9 inches).
4 In a small bowl, soften the butter, creaming it with the brown sugar. Spread this over the dough. Sprinkle with the walnuts, apricots and cherries.
5 Roll up the dough like a swiss roll, starting at the longest side.
6 Cut into nine equal pieces and place on a greased baking tray, cut-side down, to form a square, about 1 cm (½ inch) apart. Cover and leave to prove for about 30 minutes, until well risen.
7 Preheat the oven to Gas Mark 6/electric oven 210°C/fan oven 190°C.
8 Bake for 25–30 minutes, until golden brown. Place on a wire rack to cool.

APRICOT, CHERRY & WALNUT BUNS

MAKES a 20 cm (8-inch) cake
PREPARATION TIME: 10 minutes + soaking overnight
COOKING TIME: 1½–2 hours
FREEZING: recommended

IRISH BRACK

This is my brother's favourite cake and it's made from his mother-in-law's recipe.

500 ml (18 fl oz) strong tea, made using 3 teabags
225 g (8 oz) dark muscovado sugar
500 g (1 lb 2 oz) mixed dried fruit
2 eggs
500 g (1 lb 2 oz) self-raising flour

1 Mix the tea and sugar together in a large mixing bowl and stir to dissolve the sugar. Add the fruit and leave to soak overnight.
2 Next day preheat the oven to Gas Mark 3/electric oven 170°/fan oven 150°. Beat the eggs into the fruit mixture, and then carefully fold in the sifted flour.
3 Transfer the mixture into a 20 cm (8-inch) greased and lined deep cake tin.
4 Bake for 1½–2 hours until well risen and a skewer inserted into the centre comes out clean. Leave in the tin for 10 minutes before turning on to a wire rack to cool.

MAKES 8 small brioches or 1 large one
PREPARATION TIME: 15–20 minutes + rising
COOKING TIME: 15–20 minutes
FREEZING: recommended

BRIOCHES

A French sweet bread/cake, brioches can be baked whole in a deep round fluted tin or as individual cakes. We have enjoyed these for breakfast, served with unsalted butter and conserves. They can form the basis of a savoury dish, if you hollow the centre out and use the 'shell' to hold a savoury filling, or try slicing, buttering and layering into ramekin dishes to make individual bread and butter puddings.

225 g (8 oz) strong white flour
½ teaspoon salt
115 g (4 oz) unsalted butter
1 teaspoon easy-blend yeast
25 g (1 oz) caster sugar
3 eggs, beaten
50 ml (2 fl oz) hand-hot milk

1 Sift the flour and salt into a mixing bowl. Rub in the butter.
2 Stir in the yeast and sugar. Add the eggs and enough milk to make a very soft dough.
3 Cover and leave to rise for 2 hours.
4 Knead gently on a well floured surface and divide into eight pieces.
5 Take a small ball from each piece to form the 'hat'. Form the rest into buns and place in greased fluted tins. Cut a cross in the top and place the 'hat' on top. Leave to prove for 20 minutes.
6 Preheat the oven to Gas Mark 7/electric oven 220°C/fan oven 200°C.
7 Bake for 15–20 minutes, until golden. Place on a wire rack to cool.

MAKES 8–10
PREPARATION TIME: 45–50 minutes + activating yeast + rising
COOKING TIME: 25–30 minutes
FREEZING: recommended

CROISSANTS

Croissant means 'crescent' in French, hence the name of these traditional French buttery breakfast rolls.

FOR THE YEAST BATTER:
15 g (½ oz) fresh yeast
1 teaspoon caster sugar
115 ml (4 fl oz) hand-hot water

FOR THE DOUGH:
275 g (10 oz) strong white flour
½ teaspoon salt
15 g (½ oz) unsalted butter, melted
115 ml (4 fl oz) hand-hot water
150 g (5 oz) unsalted butter
beaten egg, to glaze

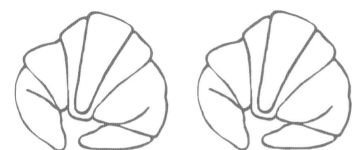

1 Dissolve the yeast and sugar in the warm water and leave to stand until frothy.
2 Sift the flour and salt into a bowl. Add the yeast mixture, melted butter and enough of the water to make a soft dough.
3 Turn on to a floured surface and knead until smooth. Cover and leave to rise until doubled in size.
4 Roll the dough into a rectangle 30 by 15 cm (12 by 6 inches). Place half the butter in small pieces over the bottom two-thirds of the dough. Fold the top third over the centre third and the bottom third up over that. Place in the fridge for 15 minutes.
5 Repeat step 4 with the second half of the butter.
6 Roll the dough out thinly and cut into triangles.
7 Starting at a long edge, roll towards the opposite point. Form into a crescent shape and place on a greased baking tray.
8 Leave to prove for about 40 minutes or until doubled in size.
9 Preheat the oven to Gas Mark 7/electric oven 220°C/fan oven 200°C.
10 Brush with beaten egg and bake for 25–30 minutes, until golden brown. Place on a wire rack to cool.

TO MAKE CHOCOLATE CROISSANTS
Before starting to roll at step 7, add a square of chocolate in the centre.

TO MAKE SAVOURY CROISSANTS
Roll a slice of cooked ham and a little grated Cheddar cheese inside in the same way.

MAKES 9 rolls
PREPARATION TIME: 30 minutes
+ resting and rising
COOKING TIME: 15–20 minutes
FREEZING: recommended

These bring back memories of summer holidays with my grandparents in Fraserburgh, when the baker's van came around on Friday and these rolls were bought for weekend breakfasts.

350 g (12 oz) strong white flour
1 teaspoon salt
1 teaspoon easy-blend yeast
1 teaspoon sugar
350 ml (12 fl oz) hand-hot water
150 g (5 oz) butter
50 g (2 oz) lard

1 Sift the flour and salt into a mixing bowl. Add the yeast and sugar. Add enough water to make a soft dough. Turn on to a floured surface and knead until smooth and elastic.
2 Place in a clean, greased bowl, cover and leave to rise until doubled in size.
3 Mix the butter and lard together and divide into three.
4 Turn the dough on to a floured surface and roll into a rectangle about 15 by 30 cm (6 by 12 inches).
5 Cover the bottom two-thirds of the dough with a third of the butter/lard mix. Fold the top third of the dough over the middle third and then the bottom third over that. Seal the edges.
6 Place the dough on a plate, cover and leave to rest in the fridge for 15 minutes.
7 Repeat stages 5 and 6 twice until all the fat has been incorporated.
8 Roll the dough into a square 1 cm (½ inch) thick and cut into nine pieces. Tuck the corners under to form rough circles and place on a baking tray. Leave to prove until doubled in size.
9 Preheat the oven to Gas Mark 6/electric oven 200°C/fan oven 180°C.
10 Bake for 15–20 minutes. Transfer to a wire rack to cool. The rolls are best served warm.

FRASERBURGH ROLLS

MAKES 12 buns
PREPARATION TIME: 40–45 minutes
+ activating yeast + rising
COOKING TIME: 25–30 minutes
FREEZING: recommended

Hot cross buns are traditionally eaten on Good Friday, the cross on the top symbolising, for Christians, the death of Jesus Christ.

450 g (1 lb) strong white flour
50 g (2 oz) caster sugar
25 g (1 oz) fresh yeast
150 ml (5 fl oz) hand-hot milk
4 tablespoons hand-hot water
1 teaspoon salt
1 teaspoon ground mixed spice
½ teaspoon ground cinnamon
100 g (4 oz) currants
50 g (2 oz) chopped mixed candied peel
1 egg, beaten
50 g (2 oz) butter, melted

FOR THE GLAZE:
50 g (2 oz) granulated sugar
3 tablespoons milk

1 Sift 115 g (4 oz) of the flour into a bowl and add 1 teaspoon of the caster sugar.
2 Blend the yeast with the milk and water. Leave to stand for 10 minutes in a warm place, until frothy.
3 Add the yeast mix to the sifted flour and sugar. Leave to stand again for 20 minutes, or until frothy.
4 Sift the remaining flour, salt and spices into a large bowl. Add the remaining caster sugar, currants and mixed peel. Mix lightly. Add the yeast mixture, with the egg and melted butter, and mix to form a soft dough.
5 Turn on to a floured surface and knead until smooth and no longer sticky. Place in a clean, greased bowl and leave to rise for about 40 minutes or until doubled in size.
6 Turn out on to a floured surface and knock back.
7 Divide into 12 equal pieces and shape each into a round bun. Place, well apart, on a greased baking tray and leave to prove until doubled in size.
8 Preheat the oven to Gas Mark 7/electric oven 220°C/fan oven 200°C.
9 Cut a cross on the top of each bun using a sharp knife. Bake for 25–30 minutes, until golden brown.
10 Make the glaze by dissolving the granulated sugar in the milk over a low heat and then boiling for 2 minutes.
11 Transfer the cooked buns to a wire rack and brush twice with the glaze while still warm.

HOT CROSS BUNS

MAKES 8–10 pieces
PREPARATION TIME: 35–40 minutes
+ rising
COOKING TIME: 25–30 minutes
FREEZING: recommended

This bread is a fusion of Mediterranean and traditional

English flavours. It's delicious served with a green salad

or a summer soup.

250 g (9 oz) strong white bread flour
½ teaspoon salt
1 teaspoon caster sugar
½ sachet easy-blend yeast
100 ml (3½ fl oz) hand-hot milk
1 egg, beaten
50 g (2 oz) butter

FOR THE FILLING:
50 g (2 oz) stoned olives, sliced
115 g (4 oz) Cheddar cheese, grated
1 egg, beaten
salt and freshly ground black pepper
sesame seeds, to decorate

1 Prepare the dough by mixing together the flour, salt, sugar and yeast in a bowl.
2 Mix together the warmed milk and beaten egg. Add to the dry ingredients and beat well.
3 Turn the dough on to a floured board and knead until smooth and elastic. Place in a clean, greased bowl and leave in a warm place to rise until doubled in size.
4 Turn the dough on to a floured surface and roll into a rectangle about 15 by 30 cm (6 by 12 inches).
5 Cover the bottom two-thirds of the dough with half the butter, chopped into small pieces.
6 Fold the top third over the centre third and then the bottom third over that. Seal the edges.
7 Turn the dough a quarter-turn and repeat with the rest of the butter.
8 Place the dough on a plate, cover and chill for 20 minutes.

MAKING THE RING
1 Mix together the filling ingredients, saving a little egg for glazing.
2 Roll the dough into an oblong about 30 by 20 cm (12 by 8 inches).
3 Spread the filling over the surface.
4 Roll the dough from the longest edge like a swiss roll.
5 Shape this into a ring. Place on a greased baking tray.
6 Make a series of cuts evenly into the ring and brush with egg. Sprinkle with sesame seeds. Leave in a warm place to rise for about 30 minutes.
7 Preheat the oven to Gas Mark 7/electric oven 220°C/fan oven 200°C.
8 Bake for 25–30 minutes, until golden brown. Transfer to a wire rack to cool.

OLIVE & CHEESE BREAD RING

MAKES 9 pieces
PREPARATION TIME: 25–30 minutes + rising
COOKING TIME: 25–30 minutes
FREEZING: recommended

These were inspired by our traditional Chelsea Buns, but have a savoury filling.

SAVOURY SWIRLS WITH TOMATO & BASIL

225 g (8 oz) strong white flour
½ teaspoon salt
25 g (1 oz) margarine
½ sachet easy-blend yeast
1 egg, beaten
5 tablespoons hand-hot milk

FOR THE FILLING:
3 tablespoons tomato purée
10 fresh basil leaves, chopped

1 In a large bowl, sift together the flour and salt. Rub in the margarine and add the yeast. Stir in the egg and milk to give a soft dough.
2 Turn on to a floured surface and knead for 8–10 minutes, until the dough is smooth, elastic and no longer sticky.
3 Place the dough in a clean, greased bowl, cover and leave to rise until doubled in size.
4 Transfer the risen dough to a lightly floured surface. Knock back and knead.
5 Roll the dough into a rectangle 30 by 23 cm (12 by 9 inches).
6 Spread with tomato purée and sprinkle on the chopped basil.
7 Roll up the dough like a swiss roll, starting at the longest side.
8 Cut into nine equal pieces and place on a greased baking tray, cut-side down, to form a square, about 1 cm (½ inch) apart.
9 Cover and leave to prove for about 30 minutes, until well risen.
10 Preheat the oven to Gas Mark 6/electric oven 210°C/fan oven 190°C.
11 Bake for 25–30 minutes, until golden brown. Place on a wire rack to cool.

This chapter represents a traditional cake from each side of 'the pond', scones from Britain and muffins from the USA. The term scone covers a wide range of fairly plain small cakes and many variations are found throughout the British Isles. Traditionally scones were cooked on a griddle, but they are now usually baked in the oven.

SCONES & MUFFINS

The American muffin is a round cake that may contain either yeast or baking powder as its raising agent. Muffins are baked in paper cases set in muffin tins ('pans' as the Americans call them) and often served for breakfast. If you run a palette knife around the top of the paper case when the muffins come out of the oven it is easier to remove the paper case once they've cooled.

MAKES about 15 scones
PREPARATION TIME: 10–15 minutes
COOKING TIME: 10–15 minutes
FREEZING: recommended

PLAIN SCONES

This is a basic scone recipe that can be used as a basis for either sweet or savoury scones. Don't over handle scone dough or attack it with a heavy hand as this will cause the dough to be tough and solid.

450 g (1 lb) self-raising flour
115 g (4 oz) block margarine
50 g (2 oz) caster sugar (for a sweet scone dough)
225 ml (8 fl oz) milk

1   Preheat the oven to Gas Mark 7/electric oven 220°C/fan oven 200°C.
2   Sift the flour into a mixing bowl. Rub in the margarine until the mixture resembles fine breadcrumbs. Stir in the sugar if making a sweet dough.
3   Make a well in the centre and stir in enough milk to give a fairly soft dough.
4   Turn on to a floured surface and knead lightly to remove any cracks.
5   Roll out to about 2 cm (¾ inch) thick and use a cutter to cut out 5 cm (2-inch) rounds. Knead the remaining dough and re-roll and cut. Place the scones on a greased baking tray.
6   Bake until well risen and golden brown, about 10–15 minutes. Transfer to a wire rack to cool.

MAKES about 15 scones
PREPARATION TIME: 10–15 minutes
COOKING TIME: 10–15 minutes
FREEZING: recommended

CHERRY & APRICOT SCONES

A colourful sweet scone to serve with coffee or tea. Delicious eaten warm or cool.

450 g (1 lb) plain flour
2 teaspoons cream of tartar
1 teaspoon bicarbonate of soda
115 g (4 oz) block margarine
50 g (2 oz) caster sugar
80 g (3 oz) glacé cherries, chopped
80 g (3 oz) ready-to-eat dried apricots, chopped
225 ml (8 fl oz) milk

1   Preheat the oven to Gas Mark 7/electric oven 220°C/fan oven 200°C.
2   Sift the flour, cream of tartar and bicarbonate of soda into a mixing bowl. Rub in the margarine until the mixture resembles fine breadcrumbs. Stir in the sugar, chopped cherries and apricots.
3   Make a well in the centre and stir in enough milk to give a fairly soft dough.
4   Turn the dough on to a floured surface and knead lightly to remove any cracks.
5   Roll out to about 2 cm (¾ inch) thick and cut out 6 cm (2½-inch) rounds with a cutter. Knead the remaining dough and re-roll and cut.
6   Place the scones on a greased baking tray. Bake until well risen and golden brown, about 10–15 minutes. Transfer to a wire rack to cool.

SERVES 8–10
PREPARATION TIME: 15–20 minutes
COOKING TIME: 20–25 minutes
FREEZING: recommended

MAKES 10–12 slices
PREPARATION TIME: 15–20 minutes
COOKING TIME: 25–30 minutes
FREEZING: recommended

FESTIVE SCONE RING

CHEESE SCONE RING

The richness of the mincemeat complements the plain scone mixture in this scone sandwich. An interesting alternative for tea at Christmas for those who are not lovers of pastry.

250 g (9 oz) self-raising flour
80 g (3 oz) block margarine
50 g (2 oz) sugar
150 ml (5 fl oz) milk
4 tablespoons mincemeat
1 tablespoon brown sugar

1 Preheat the oven to Gas Mark 7/electric oven 220°C/fan oven 200°C.
2 Sift the flour into a mixing bowl and rub in the margarine. Stir in the sugar.
3 Make a well in the centre and add enough milk to make a soft dough.
4 Knead lightly and divide into two. Roll each half into an 18 cm (7-inch) circle. Place one circle on a greased baking tray.
5 Spread with mincemeat and cover with the other half. Brush with a little milk and sprinkle with brown sugar.
6 Score the top to give 8–10 portions. Bake until well risen and golden brown, about 20–25 minutes. Transfer to a wire rack to cool.

This is delicious cut into slices and served lightly buttered. Savoury scones are traditionally cut with a plain or straight-sided cutter rather than a fluted one.

115 g (4 oz) butter
1 onion, chopped
450 g (1 lb) self-raising flour
1 tablespoon baking powder
80 g (3 oz) butter
2 tablespoons wholegrain mustard
2 eggs
150 ml (¼ pint) milk
50 g (2 oz) Cheddar cheese, grated

1 Preheat the oven to Gas Mark 6/electric oven 200°C/fan oven 180°C.
2 Heat 25 g (1 oz) of the butter in a frying-pan and fry the onion until soft and golden brown .
3 Sift the flour and baking powder into a mixing bowl and rub in the remaining butter until the mixture resembles fine breadcrumbs.
4 Stir in the cooked onion.
5 Beat together the mustard, eggs and milk. Make a well in the centre of the flour mixture and add enough egg mixture to make a soft dough.
6 Turn on to a floured surface and knead lightly. Form into a long sausage and shape into a ring.
7 Lift on to a greased baking tray, score the top several times with a sharp knife and sprinkle with grated cheese.
8 Bake for 25–30 minutes, until well risen and golden. Transfer to a wire rack to cool.

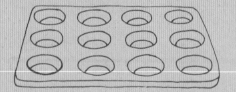 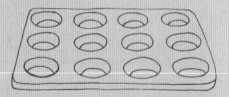 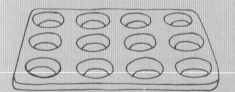

MAKES 8 scones
PREPARATION TIME: 10–15 minutes
COOKING TIME: 10–15 minutes
FREEZING: recommended

The flavour of these scones can be varied by using smoked or unsmoked bacon or pancetta.

200 g (7 oz) self-raising flour
a pinch of salt
½ teaspoon dry mustard powder
50 g (2 oz) unsalted butter
50 g (2 oz) blue Stilton cheese, crumbled
50 g (2 oz) white Stilton cheese, crumbled
2 bacon rashers, cooked and chopped
100 ml (3½ fl oz) milk beaten egg, to glaze

1. Preheat the oven to Gas Mark 6/electric oven 200°C/fan oven 180°C.
2. Sift the flour, salt and mustard powder into a mixing bowl and rub in the butter.
3. Stir in the crumbled cheeses and the chopped bacon.
4. Make a well in the centre and add enough milk to make a soft dough.
5. Turn on to a floured surface and knead lightly. Roll to 2 cm (¾-inch) thick and cut into 6 cm (2½-inch) rounds with a scone cutter.
6. Place on a greased baking tray and brush with beaten egg.
7. Bake for 10–15 minutes, until well risen and golden. Transfer to a wire rack to cool.

STILTON & BACON SCONES

MAKES 8 scones
PREPARATION TIME: 15 minutes
COOKING TIME: 10–15 minutes
FREEZING: recommended

MAKES 12 small muffins
PREPARATION TIME: 10–15 minutes
COOKING TIME: 10–15 minutes
FREEZING: recommended

WALNUT SCONES

ORANGE & CINNAMON MUFFINS

A few years ago I was asked to prepare a demonstration at Denman College on using leftovers after Christmas. This recipe was developed for that demonstration to use up walnuts. I often serve these scones with a chunky soup, made from the turkey stock of course!

200 g (7 oz) self-raising wholemeal flour
I teaspoon salt
½ teaspoon dry mustard powder
50 g (2 oz) block margarine
150 g (5 oz) Lancashire cheese, grated
50 g (2 oz) walnuts, chopped roughly
100 ml (3½ fl oz) milk
beaten egg, to glaze

1   Preheat the oven to Gas Mark 6/electric oven 200°C/fan oven 180°C.
2   Sift the flour, salt and mustard powder into a mixing bowl and rub in the margarine. Stir in the grated cheese and chopped walnuts.
3   Make a well in the centre and add enough milk to make a soft dough.
4   Turn on to a floured surface and knead lightly. Roll into a square 2.5 cm (1-inch) thick and cut into quarters and then diagonally into eight.
5   Place on a greased baking tray and brush with beaten egg.
6   Bake for 10–15 minutes, until well risen and golden. Transfer to a wire rack to cool.

Muffins are an American tradition which make a change from toast for breakfast, served with a mug of hot chocolate. The first time I came across this wonderful combination of flavours was while testing recipes for a company in America.

175 g (6 oz) plain flour
½ teaspoon ground cinnamon
1½ teaspoons baking powder
50 g (2 oz) caster sugar
grated zest of I orange
I egg, beaten
125 ml (4½ fl oz) milk
50 g (2 oz) butter, melted

1   Preheat the oven to Gas Mark 5/electric oven 190°C/fan oven 170°C. Place 12 small muffin cases into muffin tins.
2   Sift the flour, cinnamon and baking powder into a mixing bowl. Stir in the sugar, orange zest, egg, milk and melted butter, until just mixed.
3   Divide the mixture between the paper cases
4   Bake for 10–15 minutes. Press the top of one muffin lightly with your fingertip; if it feels springy the muffins are cooked. Transfer to a wire rack to cool.

MAKES 6 muffins
PREPARATION TIME: 10–15 minutes
COOKING TIME: 10–15 minutes
FREEZING: recommended

MAKES 6 muffins
PREPARATION TIME: 10–15 minutes
COOKING TIME: 10–15 minutes
FREEZING: recommended

THREE-CHEESE MUFFINS

GARLIC & HERB MUFFINS

These would be nice as part of a ploughman's lunch, to replace bread.

125 g (4^1/$_2$ oz) plain flour
1^1/$_2$ teaspoons baking powder
25 g (1 oz) white Stilton cheese, crumbled
25 g (1 oz) blue Stilton cheese, crumbled
50 g (2 oz) red Leicester cheese, grated
1 egg
115 ml (4 fl oz) milk

1 Preheat the oven to Gas Mark 6/electric oven 200°C/fan oven 180°C and place six paper cases into muffin tins.
2 Sift the flour and baking powder into a mixing bowl. Stir in the cheeses.
3 Combine the egg and milk, and stir into the dry ingredients until just mixed.
4 Divide the muffin mixture between the paper cases.
5 Bake for 10–15 minutes. Press the top of one muffin lightly with your fingertip; if it feels springy the muffins are cooked. Transfer to a wire rack to cool.

Using course-ground cornmeal (polenta) gives these muffins a lovely crunchy texture.

65 g (2^1/$_2$ oz) plain flour
^{1}/$_4$ teaspoon salt
1^1/$_2$ teaspoons baking powder
55 g (2^1/$_4$ oz) coarse cornmeal
1 garlic clove, crushed
1 teaspoon dried mixed herbs
100 ml (3^1/$_2$ fl oz) milk
1 small egg
1 tablespoon corn oil

1 Preheat the oven to Gas Mark 6/electric oven 200°C/fan oven 180°C and place six paper cases into muffin tins.
2 Sift the flour, salt and baking powder into a mixing bowl. Stir in the cornmeal, garlic and herbs.
3 Combine the milk, egg and oil and stir into the dry ingredients until just mixed.
4 Divide the muffin mixture between the paper cases. Bake for 10–15 minutes. Press the top of one muffin lightly with your fingertip; if it feels springy the muffins are cooked. Transfer to a wire rack to cool.

MAKES 16 muffins
PREPARATION TIME: 10–15 minutes
COOKING TIME: 20 minutes
FREEZING: recommended

These can be eaten by themselves or try serving them with some chocolate ice cream.

250 g (9 oz) plain wholemeal flour
4 teaspoons baking powder
100 g (3½ oz) muscovado sugar
100 g (3½ oz) shredded coconut
175 ml (6 fl oz) milk
125 g (4½ oz) low-fat spread, melted
3 eggs, beaten
175 g (6 oz) chocolate chips

1 Preheat the oven to Gas Mark 5/electric oven 190°C/fan oven 170°C. Place 16 large muffin cases into muffin tins.
2 Sift the flour and baking powder into a mixing bowl. Stir in the sugar and the bran left in the sieve. Stir in the coconut, milk, low-fat spread, eggs and chocolate chips until just mixed.
3 Divide between the paper cases.
4 Bake for 20 minutes. Press the top of one muffin lightly with your fingertip; if it feels springy the muffins are cooked. Transfer to a wire rack to cool.

NOTE: If you use smaller muffin cases, this recipe will make 30 muffins. For this size, cook for 12–15 minutes.

CHOCOLATE MUFFINS

Tray bakes are easy to prepare and they can be cut into different portion sizes, smaller ones for children and large ones for adults. They make a useful addition to lunch boxes and picnics. Children love these as teatime treats and many of these recipes are ideal for them to cook, with adult supervision. Most of these bakes will keep for a week provided they are stored

TRAY BAKES

in an airtight tin. Freezing can make oat-based bakes go soggy, however, so is not recommended, though brownies can be frozen. You will find here a recipe for Traditional Flapjacks, but also a very delicious variation which includes prunes and maple syrup – irresistible!

MAKES 9 squares
PREPARATION TIME: 10–15 minutes
COOKING TIME: 35–45 minutes
FREEZING: recommended

Brownies are a rich traditional American chocolate-based cake, eaten as a snack or for dessert. They were called brownies due to their colour and they have been eaten in the USA for about 100 years. You can store these in an airtight container for 2–3 days.

CHOCOLATE HAZELNUT BROWNIES

150 g (5 oz) plain chocolate
90 g (3½ oz) plain flour
150 g (5 oz) icing sugar, plus extra for dusting
20 g (¾ oz) cocoa powder
90 g (3½ oz) unsalted butter, melted
2 tablespoons golden syrup
2 eggs, beaten
1½ teaspoons vanilla essence
40 g (1½ oz) hazelnuts, roasted, skinned and chopped

1 Preheat the oven to Gas Mark 4/electric oven 180°C/fan oven 160°C. Grease and line the base of a 25 cm (10-inch) square baking tin.
2 Melt the chocolate in a bowl over a pan of simmering water.
3 Meanwhile, sift the plain flour, icing sugar and cocoa powder into a bowl.
4 Add the butter and syrup to the chocolate and stir until smooth. Allow to cool slightly.
5 Stir in the eggs and vanilla essence to the chocolate mixture.
6 Fold the dry ingredients into the chocolate mixture and stir quickly until smooth. Add the nuts.
7 Pour into the baking tin and bake for 35–45 minutes, until the top and edges are crusty and the inside is still gooey but not runny.
8 Leave to cool slightly in the tin. Dust with more sifted icing sugar and cut into nine squares. Serve warm with cream as a dessert or leave to cool completely, as you prefer.

VARIATION: Substitute 40 g (1½ oz) ground almonds and 1 teaspoon of almond essence for the hazelnuts and vanilla essence.

MAKES 16 flapjacks
PREPARATION TIME: 20–25 minutes
COOKING TIME: 20–25 minutes
FREEZING: not recommended

A variation on the traditional flapjack with a layer of moist fruit in the centre, this is **ideal for picnics**, lunch boxes or afternoon tea and is a real energy-booster for the young.

225 g (8 oz) ready-to-eat stoned
prunes, chopped
200 g (7 oz) unsalted butter
4 tablespoons golden syrup
2 tablespoons maple syrup
80 g (3 oz) light muscovado sugar
350 g (12 oz) rolled oats

1 Preheat the oven to Gas Mark 5/electric oven 190°C/fan oven 170°C.
2 Make the filling by heating 3 tablespoons water in a saucepan, adding the prunes and leaving to soak for 15 minutes.
3 Purée the prune mixture.
4 Heat the butter, golden and maple syrups and sugar in a saucepan, until the butter is melted.
5 Add the rolled oats and mix well.
6 Press half the mixture into a greased 18 cm by 30 cm (7-inch by 12-inch) tin. Spread the prune purée on top and cover with the remaining flapjack mixture.
7 Bake for 20–25 minutes, until golden.
8 Mark into bars and leave to cool before removing from the tin. Store in an airtight container for up to a week.

PRUNE & MAPLE SYRUP FLAPJACKS

MAKES 12 bars
PREPARATION TIME: 15–20 minutes
COOKING TIME: 30–40 minutes
FREEZING: not recommended

These are **great** for picnics and are quick and easy to make.

175 g (6 oz) ready-to-eat dried apricots
3 tablespoons orange juice
175 g (6 oz) margarine
2 tablespoons golden syrup
80 g (3 oz) plain flour
1¼ teaspoons bicarbonate of soda
80 g (3 oz) desiccated coconut
115 g (4 oz) rolled oats
175 g (6 oz) demerara sugar
grated zest of 1 orange

1   Preheat the oven to Gas Mark 5/electric oven 190°C/fan oven 170°C. Grease and line the base of a 20 cm (8-inch) square tin.
2   Place the apricots and orange juice in a saucepan and bring to the boil. Remove from the heat and leave to cool.
3   Purée the apricots in a blender.
4   In a saucepan, melt the margarine and syrup together. Remove from the heat and stir in the flour, bicarbonate of soda, coconut, oats, sugar and orange zest, mixing well.
5   Spoon half the mixture into the prepared tin. Spread the apricot purée over and smooth with a palette knife, then top with the remaining coconut mixture. Smooth the top with a palette knife.
6   Bake for 30–40 minutes, until set and golden brown. Mark into bars and cut and lift from the tin when cold. Store in an airtight tin.

APRICOT & COCONUT BARS

MAKES 16 flapjacks
PREPARATION TIME: 10–15 minutes
COOKING TIME: 20–25 minutes
FREEZING: not recommended

A favourite biscuit that is easy to make. A great store-cupboard standby and a great teatime treat for children. Keep an eye on them at the end of their cooking time as if the flapjacks are overcooked, they won't have that delicious soft texture.

200 g (7 oz) unsalted butter
6 tablespoons golden syrup
80 g (3 oz) light muscovado sugar
350 g (12 oz) rolled oats

1 Preheat the oven to Gas Mark 5/electric oven 190°C/fan oven 170°C.
2 Heat the butter, syrup and sugar in a saucepan, until the butter is melted.
3 Add the rolled oats and mix well.
4 Press into a greased 18 cm by 30 cm (7-inch by 12-inch) tin.
5 Bake for 20–25 minutes, until golden.
6 Mark into bars and leave to cool before removing from the tin. Store in an airtight container for up to a week.

TRADITIONAL FLAPJACKS

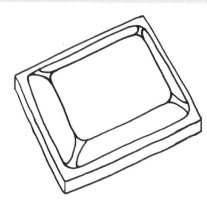 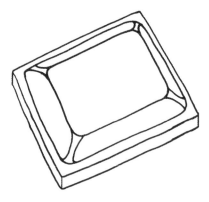 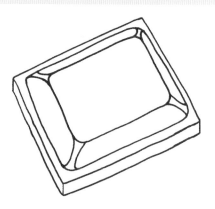

MAKES 16 squares
PREPARATION TIME: 30–35 minutes
COOKING TIME: 15–20 minutes
FREEZING: not recommended

A crunchy base is here topped with a soft peppermint icing and finished with **chocolate**.

FOR THE BASE:
150 g (5 oz) block margarine
150 g (5 oz) self-raising flour
1 tablespoon drinking chocolate
1 teaspoon baking powder
25 g (1 oz) light muscovado sugar
25 g (1 oz) cornflakes
a pinch of salt

FOR THE TOPPING:
225 g (8 oz) icing sugar
1–2 tablespoons milk
1 teaspoon peppermint essence
115 g (4 oz) milk chocolate

1 Preheat the oven to Gas Mark 5/electric oven 190°C/fan oven 170°C. Grease and line the base of a 20 cm (8-inch) square baking tin.
2 Melt the margarine in a saucepan. Mix in the remaining ingredients for the base.
3 Press the mixture into the baking tin and bake for 15–20 minutes.
4 To prepare the topping, mix the icing sugar with the milk and peppermint essence until smooth.
5 Pour the topping over the base while still hot and leave to set.
6 Melt the chocolate in a bowl over a pan of simmering water and then spread over the icing. Chill until set. Cut into 16 squares. Store in an airtight container for 3–4 days.

MINTY